The Best I Can Be
Living With Fetal Alcohol Syndrome

(Revised 2013)

by Liz Kulp

co-written by Jodee Kulp

Dedicated to:
Prenatally alcohol exposed children of the world.

At first I was mad.
Now I know I am not responsible
for getting fetal alcohol syndrome,
but I have to learn to live with it.

I think life is hard . . .
but I can't quit.

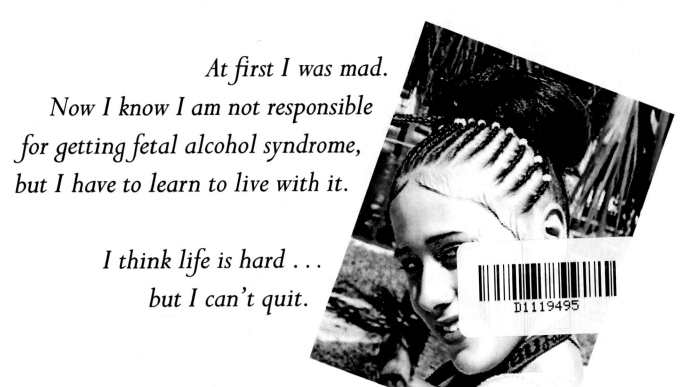

Table of Contents

Thank You

Liz and I would like to thank our Heavenly Father and all the professionals and families who are loving, working and doing research for children and persons with Fetal Alcohol Syndrome and Effects for making this book possible. We would especially like to thank the following persons for investing their time and efforts into helping Liz grow: Cathy Bruer-Thompson, Nancy Liebeg, Norman and Bev Benson, Dr. Carrie Kulp, Lauren and David Runnion-Bareford, Kathy Kienzle, Jay and Jeanne Patterson, Jeff and Kathy Haley, Greg and Dianne Olson, Robin and Jim Hokanson, Liv Horneland, JoAnn Kraft, Dr. Jeff Brist, Dr. Elizabeth Reeve, Toni Hager, Dr, Pinian-Change, Karen Johnson and the staff at www.mofas.org. We thank all the people on Faslink who have contributed quotes within the pages of this book and special thanks to Karl Kulp, Barbara Moores, Corinne Barnwell, Joyce Russell and Donna Getts.

It has been over fourteen years since we first published this book. The Best I Can Be—Living with Fetal Alcohol Syndrome or Effects (awarded best contributing young author by Mom's Choice) has been read on five continents and is used in over forty countries. It is now translated in Ukrainian and Russian.

In 2010, Liz won the Canadian Star Fish Award for having the courage to build awareness of FASDs, upon accepting this award she released her book, written in her words Braided Cord—Tough Times In and Out. Her journey and her life are just one voice of the tens of thousands of children born each year with unnecessary brain injury. We hope her life and the life of our family is an opportunity to build strength and hope for the generations following.

To Better Lives . . . Liz and Jodee Kulp
Helping others with FASDs Braid Strong Cords—May 1, 2013

Preface

It was a beautiful fall morning, the colors of the day shining into our home school classroom when Liz asked, *"Mom, do you make money on your Families at Risk book?"*

"Some", I answered, *"but more importantly the book has given hope to hundreds of families who need help loving and understanding special adopted kids like you."*

"Mom, I want to write a book about what it's like to have FAS (fetal alcohol syndrome) I think people need to know, and I need money."

Oh, Lord help me, this child is serious. I don't even know how to begin a book like this with her as the author. We're going to need help, big help! I prayed silently. A sense of quiet came over our day as I replied, *"You know what Liz? That's a great idea. I think so too. Let's find out everything we can and you can write your book. The helpers will come for us."*

And so, we sat with recipe cards and pencils and I began writing as Liz talked about what it feels like to live with fetal alcohol syndrome and we learned together. Each day we chatted while I wrote her ideas and memories and notes. The days passed and the cards stacked up. Then one day our little stack seemed complete. So, we sorted our cards into piles and saw that each pile told a story. We realized this was not just Liz's story but the story of many individuals prenatally exposed to alcohol. So, Liz began to write—her book—copying my cards. Each day she completed two cards doing her best—it is her story—the story of so many prenatally exposed children.

And, she was right—it is a story worth sharing.

"In 1999, it took Liz 30 minutes to copy two pages of this book. In 2004, she rapped and wrote poetry. Today she continues to live interdependently."

Liz age 24, adulthood with grace.

Welcome. We decided to open our family and share our experiences of living with fetal alcohol spectrum disorders (FASD). In our journey of over 26 years we have learned much. As you read this first book, "The Best I Can Be - Living with FASD", (3rd Revision) we hope that the wisdom Liz now understands as an adult can create a bridge to reach the child or person you love. Liz's dream is that the next generation of children will not be exposed to alcohol before birth and through her words and those of other families and persons living with the challenges of FASD you will come to understand the reality of this very real brain injury and subtle physical differences that occur.

May our journey bless yours - Jodee Kulp—www.betterendings.org

Let me introduce myself, I am Liz and I was born with FASD. That means my mother, for whatever reason—I will never know—drank alcohol while she was pregnant. It means before I was able to breathe my first breath—my body was already **ingesting** —that means taking into my body—alcohol. In learning more about my mother and now being an adult, I think she also had FASD. This first book, "The Best I Can Be" helps readers understand living with FASD related differences. Many of my **peers**—that means people who also have been exposed to alcohol before they were born—have been bullied by ignorant others, abused because they are misunderstood and mistreated because professionals trying to help did not understand the big picture and all those things can cause BIG problems—in our lives, in our communities and in our economy. **I gained abilities because of diagnosis.**

Living with the challenges of FASD is not easy. I must take care of my mind and body by eating well, getting plenty of sleep and not getting overwhelmed.

My fiance, Sam, also has FASD, our bodies were affected in different ways and we complement and understand each other. Sam was undiagnosed until age 33—**his courageous mother shared her truth. Together, we plan to make a difference with Live Abilities as FASD Life Experts—we take the 'dis out!**

Our family life is filled with adventures and experiences that we hope can contribute to your family's success and happiness —
Sam and I are into FASD for a lifetime!

The Beginning

Like so many stories, this tale began long ago on another fall day when life for our family was very different. It was a beautiful, crisp blue sky day that I spent walking along the lake with my younger brother, enjoying the fresh air and sharing the treasured secrets on our hearts. He was struggling with alcohol addiction and working his way through treatment. I struggled with ten years of dashed dreams trying to conceive a child. Years before my parents had faced the reality of the pain and confusion drinking caused in our family, and began renewal and restoration.

My brother still felt the aftermath of those years and his statement burned my heart, "Jodee, doesn't it make you angry at God that you can't have a child? After all, there were times it felt like you raised us." I didn't want to be childless, but my husband and I didn't feel we could make the life changes necessary to adopt an older child after fostering several children.

My heart ached as I drove home and I prayed my first sincere prayer. "Lord, send me to speak where and when you desire. My fertility and this child issue are yours." Finishing this short prayer I felt refreshed. I closed the door on barrenness, handed my fertility over to the Father and drove home under happy puffy purple and pink clouds toward a golden sunset. I left my grief in more capable hands than mine.

Our lives during that time were busy. My business was flourishing. I was chosen Entrepreneur of the Year in 1986 by the International Council of Small Business and speaking internationally on business entrepreneurship. Our design studio had won Best of Show in national competition. My clients were happy. Life was exciting and Karl and I were free to go and do just what we willed.

All this was about to change with one phone call.

> you can not see my disability on the outside.
>
> I like to make myself look pretty and I like to wear cool clothes like the other kids. people seem to notice me and I stand out in a crowd. I laugh loudly walk loudly and talk loudly. I like a good time.

Individuals with prenatal alcohol exposure often look like everyone else.

The facial differences attributed to Fetal Alcohol Syndrome (FAS) occur during only two days of gestation, so most persons affected have hidden physical and neurological differences.

Their actions and reactions to life experiences are often misunderstood.

They often have problems receiving, processing, storing and utilizing information due to neurological dysfunction.

Prenatal Alcohol Exposure is 100% preventable

While most infants are devouring information from the world around them and making neuron connections, infants exposed to drugs and/ or alcohol may be going through months of withdrawal —inability to feed, high-pitched inconsolable cries, light sensitivity, and an aversion to touch.

———

I was talking to a friend and told her what Dee had accomplished. Dee piped up, "Mom you can't expect it from me all the time now. Some days I can and some days I can't." That day everything connected right and when will it happen again? I do not know. But what I have learned is that I celebrate and empower her when she can and support the rest of the time.

Ann Yurcek, author Tiny Titan
Mom of 7 children with FASD
www.annystribe.blogspot.com

———

Jon (FASD) loves to shovel snow or dirt for the neighbors. He volunteers to bring in the garbage can or fetch things from the basement.

Bev, FASD mom

"Mrs. Kulp, we have a four-and-one-half month old, dying baby girl.
We need a licensed foster family to consider a high-risk legal adoption.
If you are interested, we will need you to fill out adoption papers."

Twelve hours after my first sincere prayer, my new life began to unfold. We hadn't filled out papers to become adoptive parents. Regardless, we were getting a child – a baby, a dying baby girl. Liz would soon join our family and life would never be the same. Who would say 'no' after ten years of waiting for a child? I decided the door to parenting a child was being flung open. In my heart and mind, the Lord had answered my prayer in his wonderful Kingly way. And, as adoption and babies often do, everything felt very miraculous. My baby, our baby was in my arms.

At that moment, my husband and I believed that love, consistency and stability changes everything. So, we poured everything we had into this special little person to undo all the damage that had been done. We didn't know how wrong we were. But we soon found out. All the love in the world can't undo the hidden damage done by alcohol to the brain and body of a small unborn child. It would be twelve and a half years before we got a diagnosis of Fetal Alcohol Effects (FAE*). Persons exposed to alcohol before birth inherit lifelong brain damage—a 100% preventable legacy.

FASD is not curable. A child does not 'grow out of it.' It manifests itself differently in each person as the alcohol attacks the tiny growing child through the bloodstream of the mother. It randomly damages many systems in the brain and/or body. The deformities for many individuals with FASD are hidden from view, making this disability even more devastating to those who live with it daily. Most persons with FASD look like the average person. Many are beautiful and some have high IQs. Researchers have not been able to come up with a one-size-fits-all diagnosis or treatment of prenatal alcohol exposure.

Today, over fourteen years later, the public awareness still needs more awareness. Liz and I hope our books, *The Best I Can Be: Living With Fetal Alcohol Spectrum Disorders (FASD)*, *Our FAScinating Journey, Keys to Brain Potential Along the Path of Prenatal Brain Injury and The Braided Cord Tough Times In and Out* can contribute to this work. **There is much work still to be done.**

*www.cdc.gov/ncbddd/fasd/facts.html—The term fetal alcohol effects (FAE) was previously used to describe intellectual disabilities and problems with behavior and learning in a person whose mother drank alcohol during pregnancy. In 1996, the Institute of Medicine (IOM) replaced FAE with the terms alcohol-related neurodevelopmental disorder (ARND) and alcohol-related birth defects (ARBD).

I'm not angry my birth mom drinking when I was in her stomach. She didn't know she was hurting me.

I am adopted and my mom died so no one will ever know when or how much or how often my mom drank. I just know it affected me and I have to live with it.

FROM LIZ ——*Just as there are many different types of drink-ers——there are various kinds of physical and neurological damage to cells of unborn children resulting from drink-ing. As an adult I know many persons who have FASD and it has been interesting to get to know each other. We find some many things the same in our experiences and the way our bodies work, even though we are each affected differently.*

You can find links and connections to meet adults living with the challenges of FASD at our website www.betterendings.org We tend to like to have a good time, we love laughing and if we were not so concentrated in our personalities

TRY THIS:

Break a raw egg into a wine glass. Add one ounce of alcohol.

Watch the clear part develop white streaks as the alcohol 'cooks' it.

Imagine these are a baby's dead and damaged cells from alcohol.

Imagine being deluged in a sea of alcohol unable to escape.

Just imagine.

What a tangled web we enter when we cross over denial into the maze of alcohol and prenatal exposure! I truly believed I left alcohol abuse behind when I began my adult life. Yet, looking back, at least five of the foster children placed in my husband and my care exhibited behaviors related to prenatal alcohol exposure. And, even though I had consumed only limited amounts of alcohol over the last 35 years, there were at least five occasions when I could have damaged an unborn child if I was pregnant. As Jesus said to the men asking for the woman to be stoned for adultery, *"Let him who has not sinned cast the first stone."* All of us, whether we have chosen to imbibe alcohol or not, need to drop our stones and walk away just as those men did 2,000 years ago.

Public understanding of prenatal alcohol exposure is beginning, and it remains commonly thought FASD happens only to the babies of poor, under educated women.

Not true! It is not only alcoholic mothers who bear prenatally exposed children. In today's western society the mothers most at risk enjoy higher household incomes, are college educated and have careers. One bout of excessive 'binge' drinking is damaging. **The damage occurs in specific cells that are developing that day and the future potential of these cells.**

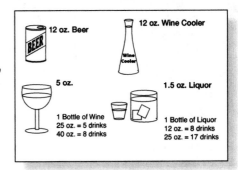

All have the same alcohol content.

When a pregnant woman drinks alcohol, so does her unborn baby. The alcohol passes quickly through the placenta into the fetus. Because the baby's systems are immature the alcohol is broken down more slowly than in the mother's body. This means the alcohol level can be higher and remain elevated much longer in the baby. **Alcohol interferes with the baby's ability to get oxygen and nourishment** for normal cell development in the brain and other body organs. What begins as relaxation for the mother deluges her child.

For these children—the damage is done—there is no undo button. Life for families of children living with FASD becomes a complex maze of isolation, misunderstanding, and twenty-four hour a day care with little or no breaks. Thankfully, early diagnosis, skillful parenting, a stable and structured home environment, a lifetime of a connected healthy community with public awareness, along with appropriate brain and body injury specific intervention can make an enormous difference in the prognosis for the person who will continue to be challenged for a lifetime. **Let Liz and our family take you on our journey inside FASD.**

Liz as an adult.

What Kinds of Damage Can Occur From Alcohol In Utero Exposure?

Primary Disabilities a child may have at birth

• Death	• Cleft palate	• ADD/ADHD Attention deficit disorders
• Height deficiencies	• Dental abnormalities	• Extreme impulsivity
• Weight deficiencies	• Immune system malfunctioning	• Sociopathic behavior
• Heart failure	• Sensory Integration	• Poor judgment
• Heart defects	• Hyper sensitivity	• Cognitive perseveration
• Renal (liver) failure	• Night terrors	• Higher than normal to dangerously high pain tolerance
• Cerebral palsy	• Sleep disorder	
• Tight hamstrings	• Precocious puberty	
• Rigidity	• Tremors	• Little or no capacity for interpersonal empathy
• Asthma	• Tourette's traits	
• Complex seizure disorder	• Autistic traits	
• Epilepsy	• Developmental delays —speech & language —coordination	• Little or no capacity for moral judgment
• Deafness		• Echolalia (repeat words without understanding)
• Central auditory processing disorder	• Mental retardation	
• Mild to severe vision problems	• Loss of intellectual functioning (IQ)	
• Dyslexia	• Little or no retained memory	
• Adaptive esotropia (cross-eyed)		
• Serious maxilo-facial deformities	• Severe loss of intellectual potential	

Sources: Malbin, Streissguth, Morse, Ritchie

What might I notice

- *Short term memory issues affects the ability to connect a behavior to a consequence and can lead to academic problems.*

- *Diverse developmental delays can affect a child in physical, social, emotional, communication, and academic.*

- *Sensory issues can affect the child's mood or behavior in specific environments—food, clothing, lighting, temperature or noise. Impulse control and inability to make predictions leads to poor social skills and safety issues.*

- *Poor boundaries may show up as overly friendly with strangers, invading another persons space or taking things that are not the childs.*

- *Difficulty in understanding abstract concepts such as time, money, or math create complications as the child gets older.*

- *Judgment skill issues make the "correct" choice more difficult to discover.*

FROM LIZ ——*People accept a person in a wheelchair, they do not say, 'get up and walk.' But people have told me, "Are you stupid, read that map!" I was too surprised to say, "You don't see my brain injury. I cannot read that map, or the telephone book, or long lists of things because they collage together. You don't know when you talk what you say to me spins in my head.*

——

I was learning how to repeat and repeat, but I didn't know my kids had a brain injury, so I just got frustrated with them. Gosh what a relief it was for me to learn and understand what alcohol has stolen from their brains and why they operate the way they do.

Terry Quinn, FASD Mom

parentingfasdkids.wordpress.com

——

FROM LIZ —— *When an idea comes into my head, I need to do it NOW! I have to keep thinking about it until I do it. I am afraid I will forget it and it will disappear—so I push and push and push until my mission or idea is accomplished.*

THE FACE OF FETAL ALCOHOL SYNDROME

Features on the left side of the illustration are considered difinitive of FAS. Characteristics on the right side are associated with FAS, but not enough to determine the presence of the syndrome. These facial features only occur during specific days in pregnancy. If a mother does not drink at that time the discriminating FAS features will not appear.

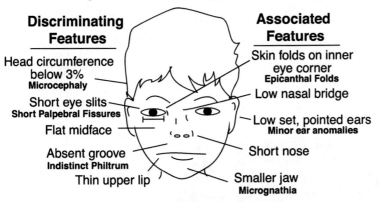

Discriminating Features

Head circumference below 3%
Microcephaly

Short eye slits
Short Palpebral Fissures

Flat midface

Absent groove
Indistinct Philtrum

Thin upper lip

Associated Features

Skin folds on inner eye corner
Epicanthal Folds

Low nasal bridge

Low set, pointed ears
Minor ear anomalies

Short nose

Smaller jaw
Micrognathia

In the young child. Streissguth and Little (1984)

The face of FAS forms between days 19-21, in most cases your child's disability will be hidden. Prepare them for encounters with authority figures.

Types of FASDs

In the United States, different terms are used to describe FASDs, depending on the type of symptoms.

Fetal Alcohol Syndrome (FAS): FAS represents the severe end of the FASD spectrum. Fetal death is the most extreme outcome from drinking alcohol during pregnancy. People with FAS might have abnormal facial features, growth problems, and central nervous system (CNS) problems. People with FAS can have problems with learning, memory, attention span, communication, vision, or hearing. They might have a mix of these problems. People with FAS often have a hard time in school and trouble getting along with others.

Alcohol-Related Neurodevelopmental Disorder (ARND): People with ARND might have intellectual disabilities and problems with behavior and learning. They might do poorly in school and have difficulties with math, memory, attention, judgment, and poor impulse control.

Alcohol-Related Birth Defects (ARBD): People with ARBD might have problems with the heart, kidneys, or bones or with hearing. They might have a mix of these.

Source: www.cdc.gov/ncbddd/fasd/facts.html, (Retrieved 04.22.2013)

In other words tens of thousand of people are born each year and are destined to live their whole lives with FASD—most invisible! A child will only have facial characteristics if the mother drank alcohol when the child's mid-face was developing during pregnancy.

———

Susan Rich and Kieran O'Malley, (2012) have proposed a psychiatric formulation based on a nuerodevelopment model to improve clinical understanding and provide appropriate treatment. This paradigm shift would better identify children who fall through the cracks and become stuck in the revolving doors of mental health and the judicial system as adults.

We will gain power in helping persons with FASD navigate today's world when we change our thinking and begin to minimize risky behaviors and reduce academic failures. When we begin to listen to the voices of the FASD Life Experts— those who live with the daily challenges of FASD. When we value the wisdom of concrete intelligence.

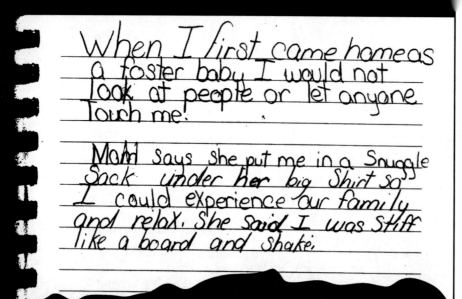

When I first came home as a foster baby I would not look at people or let anyone touch me.

Mom says she put me in a Snuggle Sack under her big shirt so I could experience our family and relax. She said I was stiff like a board and shake.

It didn't take us long to realize that this was a special child and regular parenting strategies were not going to be effective.

— ER medications to sedate aroused her.

— Cuddling sent her screaming

— Feeding, sleeping and waking were challenging for her

— Temperature change or wind created tremors

Parenting our daughter meant we had to seek insight beyond ordinary parenting books, we relied on each other and prayed for MORE wisdom.

We learned to listen to our hearts, work as a team and then use our heads to discover her needs.

How do we go on? The same way we get back on a bike when we fall, or back on a horse when we are thrown! The same way we shove one more mouthful of carrots into the mouth of a baby that is sure to spit most of it out. We know that some little part containing nourishment will stay in that reluctant little mouth! Most of all, we try to realize that every moment spent with our children helps them learn, helps them achieve, helps them know we are on their team. And then we look at our child's wonderful face and start planning tomorrow!

Lisa, FASD Mom

———

Mothering begins at conception, not at birth.

Ann Streissguth, Ph.D.

AM I TOO LITTLE TO DRINK ALCOHOL?

- A 4 wk embryo is about the size of President Roosevelt's ear on a dime.

- A 9 wk fetus is about the size of a quarter.

Liz, age four months, before joining us.

Two big brown eyes lay sullenly within a placid little face. Those two big eyes looked neither left nor right and were unable to focus or connect with another human being. Multiple moves in the child protection system provided her enough experience to know that love hurts and humans can't be trusted. At less than eleven pounds and five-months-old, Liz decided life was too hard, she was quitting. The medical profession calls this **failure-to-thrive**.

I held my new infant with the incredible love of one who had longed ten years for a child. This wasn't a cuddly baby. She bristled. Her body straightened into an unbending board. Her mouth opened and her eyes closed. We were awash in our first neurological and emotional explosion. I insisted on holding her —she resisted. We compromised by settling her into life under my large sweatshirt, riding against my bare skin in a snuggle sack. The sweatshirt provided the security she needed to experience life in our family without feeling like it was assaulting her senses. Over time she acclimated to the sounds and sensations of our home, the warmth and smells of my body, and began to accept some caregiving touch. We adapted to sleepless nights, screaming, and baby messes. She settled into rocking, singing, massages and warm baths on Mom's stomach.

Baby books would be worthless in parenting our additional needs child. Liz slept for less than two hours at a time, was a projectile vomiter, hated touch, was unattached to humans, and cried for hours. She needed more care than either my husband or I could provide. **We would need to parent from our hearts. We prayed for help and wisdom.**

Nancy with Liz, age five months, still flat affect

Help in parenting Liz has always come in remarkable ways. Our new neighbor was a registered nurse needing immediate income. She had raised five children of her own, and had the patience of a saint. Having been foster parents, we knew that keeping the adults healthy physically, mentally and emotionally was vital when working with complex children. So I returned to work part-time for my own respite, and Nancy cared for Liz.

Liz grew and began thriving under the constant intense attention and stimulation of three adult caregivers.

Liz, age seven months, after intense love and care

When I was a baby I cried alot and mom and dad had a nurse help them. her name was nancy.

I could not go into the store without getting very scared and angry.

I didnot like to be near a lot of people or noise or bright lights.
I would sit in the shopping cart and shake until I started screaming.

Living with sensory integration issues is difficult for both the child and the family. Overstimulation and/or understimulation is common with children who have been prenatally exposed to alcohol. Everyday things become big things:

- **looking at a person and sucking on a bottle at the same time**
- **clothing and shoes**
- **smells in environment**
- **daily grooming issues for hair and skin**
- **groups of people or family gatherings**
- **the sun, the wind or the rain**
- **loud or sudden noises**
- **inappropriate pain responses**
- **too soft, too hard, too cold, too hot!**

Living with FASD has giving me an advantage to be able to relate with others and to share personal experiences. I have had the opportunity to change lives. I've been able to show a positive light in the world of FASD. You don't have to go out and speak to a crowd to make a difference. You'll have opportunities all the time to educate other about FASD. Be the shining positive light the world needs to see and together we will bring the world in to the light of what it is truly like to live with FASD and the talents and strengths we have if given the love and support we all deserve.

Myles Himmelreich,
FASD Life Expert

——

Liz could not tolerate infant formula, so we worked with a clinical nutritionist to develop a nutrition program to meet her needs. Our family diet changed to permit Liz to grow. Nutrition would play a crucial part throughout her life with her sensitive biological systems. The physical issues she dealt with as an infant resurfaced in adult life and continue.

Jodee, FASD mom

Four weeks after she arrived in our home, at age six months, she made eye contact. I rejoiced! There was a spirit in this child and together we'd help it grow. Our daughter's will to live emerged and we sailed on an uncharted ocean.

Early in my understanding, I dreamt that my daughter and I were trying to get into our car to go home, but huge alligators blocked our path. Finally, just as I awoke, an alligator grabbed my finger. As I shared my dream with Teresa Kellerman (www.fasteen.com) she advised me, "Those alligators are real and are after our lives and our kids' lives. You know what? Let the alligators have that finger! It is our job to protect our kids and help them find a safe passage." In essence that is we are doing by writing this book, giving those chomping, biting, ferocious alligators our fingers in writing and getting on with loving and living our lives.

We hope within these pages we begin to provide a language of understanding so that other families can find what they need to build bridges toward safe passages. I envision that someday prenatal exposure to alcohol of our children will be a thing of the past. Until that time, our children, their families and society will have to learn to live with the complexities of FASD. **Living with prenatal alcohol exposure is difficult for everyone.**

The person exposed prenatally to alcohol may be impulsive, have limited cause-and-effect reasoning, have memory and processing issues, have difficulty understanding abstract ideas, have trouble with money, time and math, get easily frustrated, and be volatile. Faced with this set of day-to-day behaviors, many people unknowingly label the person as 'bad' instead of neurologically injured and physically inefficient.

LIZ SHARES, I am still surprised with my visits to professionals who think they communicate with me. People don't know how tolerant I am to pain. When I am hurting, it is real. When I say I don't understand, it is real. I have enough belief in myself to be my own advocate, even so I bring another person to be a cognitive translator to medical, social service, judicial and financial appointments. That person sits quietly until I signal with my body or words I need help.

It's funny to watch a professional's behavior once I ask for translation. It seems I am no longer able to see or hear or think. I become an "other" who is unable, incapable and cannot be trusted. They begin to address my translator, when it is only a blip on my brain processing.

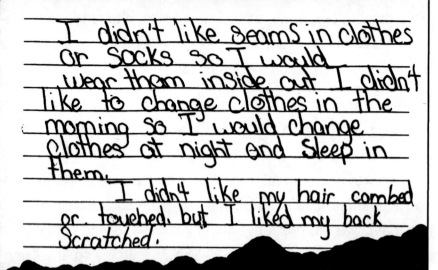

I didn't like seams in clothes or socks so I would wear them inside out. I didn't like to change clothes in the morning so I would change clothes at night and sleep in them.
I didn't like my hair combed or touched, but I liked my back scratched.

As an adult living with the challenges of FASD I can look back on my childhood to help the next generation.

Give me the freedom to be truthful with you about my differences.

- *When I ask you to show me again, say I don't remember or tell you I don't understand, please don't get frustrated. If I hide my confusion with pretend understanding it will not help either of us.*

- *I am not being shady or dishonest with you when I wear sunglasses indoors to help me see and process, I am preventing an intense headache.*

- *If I ask to eat my dinner in a bowl I have less chance of dropping or spilling. I ask for this to save your linens.*

Imagine you are in a foreign land and do not know the language. How effectively can you run your life? You may be able to ask to have your needs met, but unable to carry on a conversation.

——

The core problem of neurological damage needs to be recognized, otherwise persons with FASD are subjected to unreasonably high expectations and experience chronic failure when they don't respond to traditional therapy or are unable to learn to behave.

Teresa Kellerman
www.fasstars.com

——

As a school psychologist I often felt I was in the twilight zone, having to pick out one processing disorder over another as the main problem. In reality a whole raft of issues contributes to learning difficulties —social problems, auditory processing, memory, abstraction and organization issues. It would be much easier to call the whole thing neurological dysfunction with these features. And then look individually at each feature.

Kathy

"Hmm',I think, you have no clue" because to follow what you say, I must understand all your words and I must know your professional meanings of things like hemoglobin, renal, failure, creatinine and elevated. I must carefully watch your body language and I must fill in the places where my auditory processing has missed your vocals. I must not get anxious or worried because I do not understand you when I say, "Can you clarify and the reply is—"It means, you are impaired."

If I let my unknowing pile up I will overreact and misrepresent who I am. I will understand nothing more nor be able to ask for help. Between heartbeats my brain moves from being cooperative to being overwhelmed. My whole life I have been told—"You are impaired." My normal reaction is fight back—protect myself. Others with FASD may run or freeze up, some have learned to nod in agreement or say "thank you for telling me that" as if they understand. It keeps the peace, but does not solve anything. Others cry because it is a safer emotion and people may show kindness. That's not me—I fight to keep myself "for real"—and stable.

My translator says calmly, "you need another blood sample." A calm pours over me, I understand.

Professionals not intending to inflict harm may consider us or our parents who are providing the best parenting they are capable of to be inept. It is too easy to think, "with the proper parenting this child would be better behaved" without regard to brain injury. The diversity of professionals are like the five blind men trying to describe an elephant. One says, "The elephant is a long and flexible animal." The other says, "No, he is a round tall, animal." Another says, "No, he is hairy and bristly." Another says "He is heavy, smooth and pointy." And the last one says "He is flat and can fly." Being the person or parent standing under the rear end of the elephant, I observe they are all wrong—FASD is much more complex and encompassing. You never really know when you are going to get dumped on.

All the therapy in the world isn't going to make the brain damage disappear and misplaced treatment can increase the secondary disabilities parents work so hard to avoid. People tend to put 'normal' interpretations on FASD behavior, which makes the individual with FASD appear to be manipulative, controlling, vengeful, etc. A normal person may be able to put that much thought into something and be controlling or manipulative, but a person with FASD behavior is usually innocent impulse without restraint.

The sun really bothered my eyes. I did't like anything too hot or too cold. We live in Minnesota and it can be too hot in the summer and to cold in the winter.

I donot like any changes I would wear my bathing suit in the winter and winter coat in the summer.

Sensitivity to glare, brightness and intensity of various lighting conditions including sunlight, incandescent and fluorescent lighting may be intolerable.

Black and white contrast in text may make characters unreadable. Letters, numbers and musical notes may vibrate, shift, move and/or disappear.

Reactions include discomfort and difficulty concentrating.

Problems with spatial relationships may occur in getting on and off escalators, running and stopping, going up and down stairs, or balancing on a tile floor.

Traveling in a car with Liz was difficult. The sun bothered her eyes and she squished up her little face screaming, "Eyes, eyes." In stores, she covered her head with her blanket to avoid colors, lights, people and noise. Sensory issues affected her mood and behavior in specific environments and her preferences for food, clothes, temperature, light and noise.

Jodee, FASD mom

____

Just because a person cannot love you as you desire doesn't mean that person is not loving you with all the love they have to give.

____

I thought we were adopting a healthy, little baby. I felt so betrayed.

FASD dad

____

You cannot defend yourself and grow at the same time, either on the cellular or the body level. Your energy can be focused only on one of these functions at a time.

Julie Motz (1998)

HANGING ON FOR DEAR LIFE

Four multiple caregivers within five months, despite their love and competency, were devastating to Liz's healthy infant development. A young child can accommodate some shifting, but eventually the child gives up, suffering profound emotional and developmental loss. These issues of development and attachment further complicated the already difficult life Liz faced after conception. Still, my husband and I believed that good medical care, consistent daily schedules, one-on-one stimulation, and constant loving caregivers could meet Liz's needs.

Liz, eight months

Environment continued to be a huge battleground. Liz was tactile defensive which means she was hypersensitive to touch, light, sound, smells and movement. Even at age seven, if we touched, brushed up against her or physically directed her to safety, she screamed, **"Owie you're hurting me. Stop hurting me."** How could normal loving touch feel painful to her? Why did she shove or push us away? Only her beloved blanket 'Gee' protected her and she securely bundled herself to settle into our laps for comfort, songs, stories and reading.

Her favorite early childhood outfit was a diaper or panties. Her preferred hairstyle was unwashed and unkempt. We chose clothes based on softness, flexibility and comfort. We removed labels and turned clothes inside out. We avoided cuffs and elastic and devised alternatives for mittens and boots by using Daddy's big warm woolen socks over-velcro strapped shoes. It made no sense to fight with laces. We found a soft, warm, fuzzy rabbit fur hat to keep little ears from freezing.

At each turn in our FASD journey we encountered rough terrain where we needed to build bridges and make detours to create a semi-normal life. Crowded spaces, elevators, standing in line, tents or the backseat of the car enclosed her and she felt crushed. Sunlight glistening off the snow or fluttering through the trees overstimulated her eyes. Loud noises and background conversation caused her to cover her ears.

Overwhelmed meant overreaction and we learned when we managed Liz's environment we enjoyed a bright eyed, happy child. My dreams of library visits, children's museums, art fairs and circuses were replaced with a romper room of home-based controlled stimulation. We exposed her to new and varied experiences in small bits knowing someday she must learn to live in the chaos of the adult world and still enjoy life.

We needed to focus on creatively rearing this child to raise an adult.

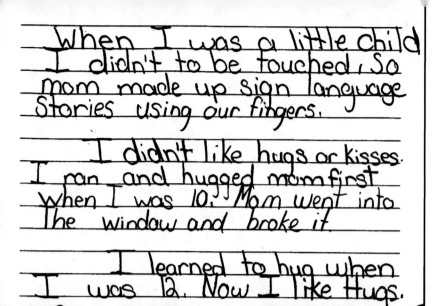

When I was a little child I didn't to be touched, So mom made up sign language stories using our fingers.

I didn't like hugs or kisses. I ran and hugged mom first when I was 10. Mom went into the window and broke it.

I learned to hug when I was 12. Now I like Hugs.

Liz was touch adversive and we used finger play stories to touch wiggly toes, rub her back, massage arms and legs and lightly stroke her face and hands. The Teddy Bear Garden and Little Turtle were two of her favorites.

We spent hours writing letters and numbers on her back while she guessed secret messages. We used pure essential oils—lavender and chamomile—to massage her muscles. Games allowed us to initiate healthy touch.

Some children with FASD may seek inappropriate or excessive touch.

As an infant, Liz held her hands in tightly locked and closed fists when overwhelmed. I'd stroke the top of her hand and tell her, "Your hand looks like a little turtle. Can I take a journey to find her sister turtle who lives on the other side of your noggin.'"

She always nodded and slowly I marched my fingers zigzag up her arm, stopping at the elbow, "Do I still have permission to find the sister turtle?" Then my fingers tapped up her arm, over the shoulders, up her neck to the top of her head.

"Can I go down?" I asked. "This is treacherous and you are brave!" I lightly marched around her mouth, nose, ears and closed eyes asking, "Have you seen sister turtle?" She shook her little head. Then I'd journey down her other arm watching as she relaxed and a smile crept on her lips.

At the bottom, the little turtle (her thumb) popped out along with an "I did it" grin and for a brief moment I could hug the whole child!

OVERSTIMULATION – SHOPPING TIL LIZ POPPED

As a person with tactile defensiveness, Liz is very sensitive to random movement. She told us stores, schools and clinics made her head crazy. More than once I left a full shopping cart to attend to the more important needs of my child. One minute she was calm and smiling. The next minute she exploded into an episode of uncontrolled screaming—these were limbic rages and not temper tantrum.

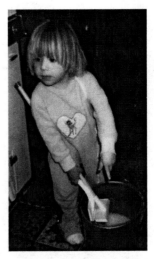

Liz began building life skills as a toddler—cleaning, cooking, and house care.

We practiced movement with wooden wagon rides, packed with her blankie, 'Gee', her beloved little brother, David, and three harnessed wonder doggies. When she felt life was getting overstimulating, we taught her to stop, close her eyes and say *"Stop, Focus, Control."* One day in the store, two-year-old Liz held onto the shopping cart, her body shaking, eyes squeezed tight, fists clenched, shouting *"Control me! Control me! Me control me!"* Store patrons walked quickly past glaring at me. The difference in our understanding of the situation was chasms apart—I, proud of my darling daughter working so hard to cope with sensory issues—the public looking away, finger pointing and staring as the judge and jury. We quickly checked out.

Liz's response behavior is magnified ten-fold compared with other children. We called it accelerated normal. It may not be unusual for a child to take free colorful chocolate suckers and stick them in her underwear to free hands for other experiences. The FASD highlights came into play after the chocolate melts in the underwear in a gooey mess and my tactile defensive child hates the feeling. It magnifies to horrific proportions when Mom adds cool water to the goo in a public washroom and hardens the candy pulling her skin tight. I expected social service sirens at our nuclear meltdown.

It was twelve years before we understood the roots of her dilemmas, the cause of anxiety in school and her store headaches. We didn't know that Liz felt and heard fluorescent lights buzz. They made her world dance and she tried to avoid them. In our home we switched to 'full spectrum' fluorescent which were significantly less troublesome for her. Liz learned to be assertive in clinic and group environments regarding her lighting needs and even today she may wear sunglasses to the dental office or colored contact lenses to dim the light. We worked with a developmental optometrist and neurodevelopmentalist who taught us eye exercises to help Liz's eyes function better with various common lighting. With the correct therapy at age thirteen, she no longer flipped out and popped in the store. She shopped.

Family parties too noisy and busy.

I would add more noise and get busy to. It felt like I was a wind up toy, dad would say "who put a quarter in you?"

When we went to family parties mom and I would go little hiding corner to be alone.

We arrived late and left early . . .
We practiced STOP.

Stand still
Think
Observe
Protect yourself

We role played in advance for holidays and special occasions.
We advised friends and relatives of our child's specific needs.

TIP FROM LIZ: Please wrap my gifts simply. Tape and ribbons frustrate me and by the time I have opened the gift— I am less appreciative. Gift bags or a stocking are great!

"Crowds and large gatherings cause a lot of stress. I have a hard time mingling and fitting in. I feel awkward, like a lost needle in a haystack, over-whelmed with nothing to say. Put me with 3 or 4 people I'm "OK." I can interact and share. I've been this way all my life. I still believe I don't have much to offer to the conversation!"
Steve—FASD Life Expert, author
The Long Way to Simple

———

Liz wants to behave like other children. She cannot see beyond the moment or past a situation. She reacts 'out-of-control'—the only way she is capable of, when stressed or overloaded. After, she has had time to calm down and regroup, I provide her with new ways of coping and we role play with Plan B for next time.

Jodee, FASD mom

———

FROM LIZ— Know that it takes me longer to understand new events, new places and new peo-ple. When all of these things happen at the same time it can be over-stimulating and overwhelming. When I have to deal with too much new, my body does not function as well and that is when I get hurt.

FAMILY GATHERINGS

Large family gatherings, relatives visiting or friends over for dinner overstimulated Liz. The traditions we embraced with fondness sent Liz into a tailspin—disrupting the security of her routine. Projects and celebrations we rejoiced in exhausted her. Her surrounding environment was steeped in distractions. People she didn't know or recognize expected her to react like other children.

We found ourselves dodging friends and family. We hid in out-of-the-way nooks and crannies in their homes to soften the stimulation and yet experience the feasts and celebrations. We dined under a table peering out beneath the table cloth. We ate our dinner in the quietness of a bathroom, enjoying fine dining on a furry toilet seat cover.

Many times we huddled in the coat room listening to muffled conversations, rapped in our blanket friend 'Gee', while Liz regrouped. I sang softly the songs of the season. In the homes of our dearest friends, Liz sometimes took a hot bath and snuggled sleepily in my arms. Finally, Mom enjoyed evenings of adult conversation, something very rare during the early days of raising Liz.

I tried to imagine what it must be like. I sat on the floor with my eyes closed, trying to listen to all twelve conversations at one time, feeling very small and overwhelmed. My child was a stranger in a strange land, unable to separate languages or sequence change.

The electrical storms in Liz's brain caused meltdowns. These rages are often misinterpreted as willful disobedience or temper tantrums. In reality, the person with FASD has little or no control over the experience once it begins. The surrounding audience's best defense is keeping the individual safe and minimizing the destructive forces of the tornado within. After a rage, Liz had no idea regarding her behavior. She was sweet as could be. Onlookers remained stunned as my heart pumped loudly. Verbal escalation on our part or physical restraint of Liz increased the duration of the rage and we learned to move her into a safe, quiet space and monitor. If we could not move her, we talked to her softly and encouraged eye contact. To others, it appeared like complete marshmallow appeasement and they believed her behavior to be our fault. They believed we lost control when in reality we were maintaining control.

As Diane Malbin so rightly states—**parent differently not harder.** Karl and I questioned how many abused children are prenatally affected.

Mom would sing and rock me and tell stories. before bed. I had night terrors and I would run through the house Screaming and crying and talking.

I would take warm bubbly baths before bed to help me go to Sleep. Mom would use the drying machine to get me dry.

Imagine you are sitting on a very hard chair that is too small for you so your body is compressed.

. . . The floor is moving ever so slightly.

. . . The lights in the room are flashing.

. . . There is a ringing alarm clock and a humming sound that seems to never end.

. . . Your friend is talking to you, but you only are able to understand every third or fourth word.

. . . Then your dog jumps upon you with kisses after being sprayed by skunk.

Now imagine you have no control over any of this. You cannot get away. People are moving and talking faster, and faster, and faster.

Imagine.

After she napped, Liz often awoke disoriented and screamed for 45 minutes. Once she regrouped, she'd hop off my lap, smile, run and play as if nothing happened. I was left behind exhausted.

Nancy, Liz's RN Nurse

————

Keeping Liz safe at night was a concern. She often awoke from a deep sleep screaming. Then she walked through the house terrorized, shaking and crying followed by our beloved doggies. We comforted her and directed her back to safety. She never remembered the experience. Once on vacation she escaped from our condo and walked into a nearby condo, her parents fast on her heels. Our door had been locked.

Jodee, FASD mom

————

FROM LIZ —— Even as an adult I am unable to nap. I have the worst nightmares you can imagine or am unable to wake. As an adult, I take medication to help me sleep. Without sleep I do not function well.

PICKING OUR BATTLES

Changes in weather remain difficult even as an adult.

Transition time for a person with FASD is often very difficult. A change in routine can send them over the edge. If we placed normal expectations on Liz any situation could become a battle Changes in weather, bedtimes and morning times were especially trying. Changing clothes topped her list of frustrations and jammies after baths were impossible. We developed gentle bedtime rituals to help limit her night terrors. We said good night to the day with a warm bath and wrapped her in a soft terry towel. I rubbed her tiny body dry, and she settled enough to let me dry and brush her frazzled hair while I sang children's songs. We rolled her in 'Gee' and piled covers on top of her. In the corner of her bedroom tiny Christmas tree lights twinkled. We snuggled together reading and sharing daily adventures to reinforce what she had learned. She slept in her most comfortable jammies—her blanket 'Gee.' Eventually, she fell asleep—never for long.

Liz's Adoption Day - 14 months with Mom and Dad.

I heard Liz's ear-piercing scream as I lifted a shovelful of three-foot deep snow after a Minnesota blizzard. Liz flew out the door and through the air as she frantically looked for us. Her naked body landed neck deep in the snow. At bedtime we told her to go to the window and wave to us when she awoke. She didn't remember. For two hours, she cried as we held and comforted her. She melted into our arms for the first time shedding feelings of abandonment. She was developed enough to attach words to feelings. She was almost seven-years-old.

Liz has always been a unique problem solver. From that point on, to avoid the morning clothes transition, she wore her next day's outfit to bed. It took until age thirteen before a pair of flannel pants and a big polar fleece shirt served as pajamas. It took until later in her teen years before she enjoyed picking out morning clothes.

FASD families need to be creative and flexible in the little daily issues. Some families adjust by making the form of a person on the floor with the child's clothes before going to bed. The child just jumps into them upon arising. Others heat clothes in the dryer and challenge the children to jump in before they get cold.

Mom and Nancy read me hundreds of stories, we did lots art and puzzies. They taught me to caant but I told them they didn't Know the right way. It was 1.2.3.5.6.7.9.10 For you for me is not a number and I ate my dinner.

Everyone thought I was Smart. I knew 60 breeds of dogs when I was three and all my colors when I was two. I knew all the words to songs and sang all the time.

Over time we got past most of the attachment issues. Still there were missing pieces.

She seemed to live in a world apart. My heart struggled watching her watch other children who did things she was unable.

She couldn't cut, hop, or skip.

I couldn't figure out how to teach her. teaching her was very difficult. It was like filling a bucket full of holes. As fast as the information went in, it seemed to pour out.

When Liz was three, we had three loving standard poodles, each with very different personalities. Abraham, our jet black male, had just absconded with something he thought was delightful. My husband caught him and stated, "That dog needs jail!" "Daddy, what does Isak need?" Liz asked. "Well, Isak needs consistent parenting or he gets into trouble." "What does Joey need?" she continued. "Joey just needs love, he always wants to be good. What kind of parenting do you need Liz?" "I need attention parenting!" she loudly declared.

Jodee, FASD mom

———

When Dee said "I forgot", I realized that she did forget. It took until she was 17 for others to understand that. When she told me that she was "bored", she didn't know what to do next! When she fought me with a chore, "it will take forever" she was overwhelmed or confused about what to do. Translated— it was too much, too long, and too confusing. Solution—The only way to do it was to support her and encourage her.

Ann Yurcek, author, FASD Mom to 7, Tiny Titan

ANIMALS PAVED THE WAY TO AFFECTION

Animals are a large part of our family life. We instill in our family members the need to care deeply for all creatures using gentleness, consideration and kindness; tempered with structure, rules and obedience. We've trained some wonderful animals playfully with love and kindness. I was not surprised when my dear friend Liv said, *"Jod, if you can get through to those animals—you can reach Liz."*

Liz has always had unique relationships with animals.

We hand-raised tiny wild baby bunnies and returned them to the Owl Forest. We watched scoops of tadpoles grow into frogs in our kitchen and then sadly jump into Sunday morning orange juice. Birds built their nests outside our school window. A friendly Siamese Fighting Beta fish swam in a lighted tank to protect children needing to use the toilet in the night. Liz raised baby chicks and ducklings that sweetly perched on her shoulders. Two African frogs lived in Liz's room for five years!

Age ten is when most children move from concrete to abstract academics. For children with FASD who often never acquire abstraction this change in their school and peer relationships is devastating. Stuck in earlier child thinking and playing, their friends move on in new interests of study, play and humor. It is the beginning of a new loneliness. Our friend Greg, of Critters and Company was given an abused cockatiel who had been evicted from five homes due to obnoxious bird behavior. Feisty 'Emily' reminded Greg of Liz. After he cleared it with Karl and me, he talked Liz into taking the bird on as a challenge. He explained to her that the bird had behaviors he saw in her—hissing, biting, jumping up and down, and squawking. Since she knew how it felt to have those behaviors, perhaps she could help the bird behave better. It was her job to help the bird become a better bird. Liz's new title was 'Animal Trainer.' Our new parenting job was to protect the bird.

One day I watched in amazement as a yellow-feathered, eight-inch bird and a frustrated girl jumped up and down, hissed, spat, squawked and screamed at each other, neither of them budging from her own vantage point. The scene was comical and I thought *"Dear God, is that how I look to You when I yell at Liz?"*

Over time, the bird and the girl became loving to each other. Liz wanted the bird to allow her to touch it. This desire allowed us to share how we also felt when she didn't want us to touch her. Soon after, Liz told me she loved me. Shortly after, she hugged her father for the first time. **He had waited ten long years.**

> I me morized the alphabet song but couldn't put it together. The letters kept dancing on the paper.
>
> Why wast b,d,p,q all the same. They looked the same to me, so did u,n,m, and 3, 7, 1 and 6 and 9, 5 and 2. I didn't know why you had to read one way left to right when you could read right to left too. I still have trouble knowing right and left sometimes.

Liz's wisdom often startles me with its logic. I so wish I could see her mind work with its unusual circuitry—I must ask myself 'how does this make sense'? It usually does.

To Liz, the letters b, d, p and q were all the same. For her whole life a pen had remained a pen. A car had remained a car. Now we were telling her that a line and a circle placed differently were different letters and this did not compute. If she could walk both directions, why couldn't she read both directions?

I asked if more letters were "WRONG" for her.

And she replied, "3, m, w" and "7, r, L". The kid had obviously been doing her homework!

Liz's world view is very different from how I live life. As we remediated ten-year old Liz's reading skills we discovered information from one part of her brain had difficulty connecting to information in another area of her brain. She spelled well during spelling lessons, then ten minutes later the material she knew evaporated and she could not to read the same words in a sentence. Liz knew she had understood this only moments before and her frustration escalated. Whose wouldn't?

Each gift of knowledge felt to her as if it was being stolen and I did not understand I would need to teach the same material in many locations, under many situations and things like lighting, smell, temperature, wind variances were just as detrimental to her retention as was sleep, food, stability, distraction and stress.

No wonder she knew her spelling words in our dining room and not at school!

A ROMPER ROOM HOME

During Liz's early childhood we shared our home with a number of infant and toddling foster children. David joined us at eight-months-old. An infant stroke left him paralyzed on one side and social services knew he had been prenatally exposed to alcohol. Because David was unable to use one side of his body we held his good side and encouraged him to utilize his weak side. He cross-pattern crawled to reach Cheerios we placed on stairs and ladders. His favorite daily event and first word was "hot tub." He happily splashed and swam as Karl held his good side. Our knowing about David's early brain injury made significant impact in his later growth and development and adult outcomes.

Dave and Liz's wagon pulled by three beloved doggies

Liz (3) and David (15 mo.)

Indoors we built obstacle courses addressing both children's needs for walking, crawling, jumping and climbing. Sofa cushions, pillows and blankets became mountains and tunnels strewn helter-skelter to encourage exploration. My husband cut peg board into one-foot squares so we could lace them together to make boxes and tunnels. Cupboards were emptied and refilled with pans and bowls. We filled containers with beans, rice and other pouring things for tactile exploration. We brought snow inside in dishpans to build snowmen when it was too cold. We filled sinks with bubbles and water. We washed and re-washed toys in water play. We poured, and dripped, and dropped, and mopped. We spent hours playing with puzzles, and stringing, lacing, and building. We read, played house, danced and sang.

Outdoors we built sandboxes, garden paths, an airplane tree house and wooden play systems. We stomped in puddles, rolled in leaves, hiked in the magical forest, and enjoyed nature. We swung on the porch swing and lazed in the hammock. We dug worms and played in the earth. We watched birds, ants and any other critter that came our way. We bundled up in the red wagon and marched around the neighborhood pulled by our wonder doggies.

Unlike Liz, David thrived on affection and positive touching. He loved being held and cuddled. He and Liz developed a brother and sister bond continuing today. At fifteen months a secure, happy and walking David ran. At seventeen months he had twenty-five clear words and discerned multiple motor sounds. He put the correct pieces into wooden puzzles. At three, Liz knew sixty breeds of dogs, beat us in putting her puzzles together and loved using "Daddy's big words." She loved listening to stories and playing with David.

Then David moved on, as foster children do.

I wanted to go to school. I thought it would be fun. I liked Kindergarten. I had a good teacher.

But in first grade, I felt dumb. I asked questions and everyone laughed at me.

I always had to sit by the teacher Everyone could read and I couldn't.

The teacher wrote too fast on the board and I could never catch up.

I did not want to be there.

Kid's would tease me and say I was the kid with only 10 spelling words ha ha!

Thinking and learning are not all in our head. On the contrary, the body plays an integral part in our intellectual processes.

Research shows that there is a connection between activity and levels of alertness, mental function and learning.

S.M.A.R.T. stands for Stimulating Maturity through Accelerated Readiness Training
A Chance to Grow's new affordable brain training curriculum for Pre-K, Ages 3-5 (www.actg.org)

I tried the college thing and always failed. I learned it's okay. I am not a highly educated college person. I have to work hard for a little money. Without me people wouldn't look as good. I can't be what I wasn't born to be.

Fran, FASD Life Expert

—

FROM LIZ —— *I soon became known as the kid who had only 10 spelling words—ha-ha-ha. The kid who can't read. Kids didn't know they were tearing my heart out by their statements. I was trying my hardest and I couldn't do it. Eventually I started being mean back.*

—

Liz had great difficulty in:

- *Retrieving previously stored information.*
- *Making associations.*
- *Comparing and contrasting.*
- *Forming generalizations.*
- *Seeing similarities and differences.*
- *Understanding cause and effect.*
- *Walking the walk after talking the talk.*
- *Turning hearing into behavior.*
- *Doing immediately without thinking.*

SCHOOL EXPERIENCES

Liz adapted well socially and enjoyed the crafts, stories and playtime with other children at a small preschool. We enjoyed the respite. Preschool screening determined Liz would benefit from another year at home to catch up on gross motor and auditory processing skills. So Liz remained home and went to preschool again and her friends moved on.

We searched for a small kindergarten and found a school of only eighty children in grades K-8. Her teacher was incredible and the children were well-behaved and bright. Liz entered kindergarten at age six, still unable to cut out shapes, hop or skip. While the children practiced memorization, Liz stared out the window. While the children sang, Liz looked at the floor. While the children wrote alphabets, Liz scribbled. But, she excelled at recess and with her outrageous personality she made friends!

First grade was the beginning of a downhill slide. Liz finished kindergarten on a high note. She was excited to attend first grade. We spent the summer playing school and practicing letters and numbers. She boarded the bus the first day feeling secure.

She used her 'big Daddy words' during story time. Then she discovered she couldn't learn to read. Her letters danced on the paper. The other children laughed at her. Her desk was placed next to the teacher to get special help. She began copying other children's papers trying to grasp what was going on. Her teacher grew more and more frustrated. "Is she lazy? Why can't she learn?" Journal entries from her first grade teacher include, "I told Liz yesterday that 'I forgot' is not a good excuse." "Liz seems sad and said unkind things to another student, I hope she is not jealous she is struggling so to read."

Arriving home after school, Liz slammed the door, threw her backpack on the floor and exploded. She quit masquerading as a 'normal' school child. The pressure of the school day released into a snarling, growling, screaming, crying mass on my kitchen floor. I began to daily document behaviors and statements. We played school before dinner trying to learn what the other children had learned during the day. Our bright-eyed, sparkling daughter who had come so far, now spent story time curled up in a fetal position. We asked for an assessment, but she was not far enough behind to qualify for special programs. We considered homeschooling and having Liz attend school half days. Her school was very accommodating, but was concerned that her needs were more than they could meet. Liz began to get stomach aches and headaches. Her beloved storybooks became her enemies and she no longer wanted us to read to her at bedtime. School became a nightmare.

Grandma reading to Liz

When I was little I wanted to play harp. I still play but I had a real hard time.

Mom wouldn't let me quit. She says it helps my math. She says I need to learn I can't quit hard things. I think life is hard, but I can't quit.

Mom says I am important and God has a plan for my life.

The goal of Talent Education is the development of a 'noble heart'. Special features of the Suzuki Method include:

- *Parent involvement*
- *Listening*
- *Repetition*
- *Encouragement*
- *Learning with other children*
- *Early beginnings*
- *Graded repertoire*

Much of what I learned in teaching Suzuki I carried over to other subjects. This method of teaching was our first clue to help Liz.

Suzuki's most important lesson was . . .
Master and love each tiny step by tiny step !

Dr. Suzuki developed his method to help children fulfill their capabilities as human beings, not to produce professional musicians. Playing an instrument did not come easily for Liz. We taught her only three to four notes and one tiny new thing at a time. The Suzuki method breaks each song into hundreds of learning opportunities so we could focus on many different things within pieces she already knew.

We provided rewards for:

- a positive attitude
- trying something new
- practicing pieces
- attending musical events

Liz enjoyed group lessons until she discovered that six year old children who began harp instruction two years after her, had moved beyond her skills. Tremendous love and respect of each child is central to the way in which teachers and parents work together within the approach. It is another way of making a major contribution to the life and growth of the child.

It emphasizes cooperation, and for the child to be the best person the individual can be.

SUZUKI — THE ART OF LISTENING

Liz loves music. As a small child she laid on the couch and told us her ears were "eating the music and putting it into her tummy." Liz's older cousin plays beautiful harp music and inspired Liz to to play the harp. We decided to introduce Liz to harp music instruction with the Suzuki method.

Liz was not able to play with two hands until she could cross her midline

Dr. Suzuki believed musical ability is not an inborn talent, but a talent that can be developed. Any child properly trained can develop musical ability in the same way most children learn to speak their mother tongue. The potential of every child is unlimited and in teaching the child music, we are creating a medium for emotional and spiritual growth. As he said, *"Teaching music is not my main purpose. I want to make good citizens, noble human beings. If a child hears fine music from birth, and learns to play it himself, he develops sensitivity, discipline and endurance. He gets a beautiful heart."*

The ideas of parental responsibility, encouragement, listening, and constant repetition are some of the special features of the Suzuki method. The parents become the 'home teachers' and learn to play and teach the child. The child's efforts to learn are met with sincere encouragement. Each child learns at a individual rate, building on small steps to master each step. There is no set time plan to the learning. The general atmosphere is enjoyment, generosity and cooperation. Steps are repeated continuously throughout the program to provide reinforcement. Each child plays the same repertoire of music encouraging younger children to play what older children are playing. In addition, Suzuki students develop basic competence on their instruments before they read music.

Children as young as three or four-years-old learn to play an instrument by ear using the Suzuki program. Liz was already seven, far older than most of the beginners and struggled with auditory processing deficits. We wrote to MacPhail School of the Arts in Minneapolis and provided details about Liz and her desire to play. They blessed our family with an instructor who was the first chair harpist from the Minnesota Orchestra willing to do private instruction in her home to decrease stimulation. The skill of teaching three and four-year-olds blended well with finding ways to creatively teach Liz. The hard work of learning music strengthened the paths between the right and left hemispheres of her brain and improved listening skills.

As an adult, noble Liz has a fine ear for music—she spent six years in Book One.

I liked recess The best because I was free to play with my friends. The School food was not good for me, but I would get sick after I ate.

The lights in The School gave me headaches. I could see The light flicker and it made my head crazy. Today I take Special vitamins to help me with the light and I wear Sunglasses at the dentist when I have to look at those lights.

Everyday I had head aches, and Stomach and would get dizzy.

Parents of children with FASD can help disprove the dysfunctional family theory by:

- **Attending parent/teacher conferences**
- **Becoming active in the child's class**
- **Volunteering in the school**
- **Attending school activities**
- **Consistently communicating with the school and your child's teacher**

Braid others into the life of your child and find ways to you can become active in your child's life—scouts, place of faith, sports.

Normal brain development is orderly and sequential. Rich neural networks provide opportunities to link, integrate, and associate. Persons with FASD have fewer physical links for retrieval, integration and other options. Spotty learning and retrieval is normal; strengths may be atypical. As with all people, people with FASD are always learning, but may require specific cues to access previously stored information.
Barbara Morse, Ph.D. (1991)

FROM LIZ —— *I wish someone would have realized in first grade when my headaches and stomach aches began that there were things we could do to help me manage the stress and anxiety I felt everyday in school. As an adult, I have spent two years in physical therapy learning things I could have already known.*

We decided that public school, with its wide array of services and diversity of teachers was a better option. Liz's new second grade teacher had been a special education teacher in a senior high school and was exceptional. Liz's hand-picked public school third and fourth grade teachers were just as skilled. It wasn't an issue of teacher quality—something was very different and complex with our child. And the labels were piling up!

When other children were learning to read, Liz was struggling with a dancing alphabet. While others were beginning to write stories and short reports, Liz coped with coloring, using a scissor and getting her letters to stay on the line. While others sang "Go You Chicken Fat Go" and exercised, Liz struggled coordinating words with impossible actions. Finally, two years behind, she qualified for an assessment and began Title 1 services for reading and math to help her catch up with other students. Yet even with supports and excellent teachers, information learned yesterday was forgotten today. Her numbers and letters were transposed. The child who worked so hard to love life no longer contributed anything in class, her eyes sullen, her face expressionless.

FROM HER FOURTH GRADE REPORT:
"Elizabeth often makes disparaging remarks about herself. She misread words she did know, and then argues about what she had said. Constructive correction is received negatively. In spelling 18 cvc and 2 silent e words, Liz had 25% accuracy. She did

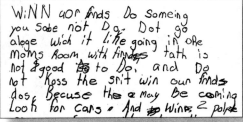

Liz's handwriting at the end of 4th grade.

not use /th/ or consonant blends correctly. She often used the short vowel and then added another vowel in error. In math Liz was fairly accurate using her fingers for computation in addition and subtraction. She demonstrated knowledge of multiplication and division. In reading, she falls below the 16th percentile. Giving her positive comments is very productive. It is also beneficial to let her self-correct rather than marking something wrong."

Liz compared herself to classmates. She thought she was stupid. She hated reading. She hated school. She hated herself. She struggled in group environments. At home, she fell to the floor in rages, used vulgar language and spoke to her family by shouting. Headaches, stomach aches and dizziness occurred daily. She continued to gain weight. She was a very unhappy child. A complete medical exam discovered nothing unusual. Liz, however, compensated for her educational defeats with 'friendships.' Her sense of humor, fascinating playroom and our Minnesota winter hot tub moved her to celebrity status with her peers and if 'friends' asked her to do something she did it.

I always have lots of friends we liked to have races. I was a fast runner and could win.

I like playing with friends. Our family does fun things, and my friends like being here. We have a hot tub and we had a trampoline. But then mom said too many kids and the trampoline went away.

We also go on bike rides to get ice cream. I like riding bike.

Though outgoing and socially engaging children with FASD are often impulsive, intrusive, overly talkative, hyperactive and starving for attention.

- **Limited social adaptation is a common problem.**
- **Poor judgment leads to exploitation, isolation and establishment of few true friendships, even though they may be surrounded by persons they consider 'friends.'**

It is not uncommon for a child to call a list of friends for a play date—and all answer NO!

By the age of nine or ten most children are socialized to cultural norms. Liz was still a toddler on a huge adventure. You never knew what direction she'd dash. I felt isolated as I tried to protect Liz from the world and the world from Liz. We decided, it was time for a change. Liz would not become handicapped because I was protecting her; she'd have to learn to manage in society. I needed to learn the difference between in "able" and enable. That was going to be a long hard journey.

Most children with FASD have trouble taking in verbal instruction, processing the information, remembering what is expected of them and then completing a task. They find it very difficult to master social skills without explicit concrete direction. The next years would mean intense instruction if Liz was to be safe and gain adult interdependence. I found no book or road map to tell me what to do so I began charts and notes and data that I could cross reference to find a path.

By age nine our dreams of academic success for Liz had been crushed. Her bad behavior was escalating and we were concerned institutional placement loomed on the horizon. We didn't have the money to choose to homeschool and yet it seemed the only option. Liz's teachers were not the problem— they were excellent. I knew Liz was able to learn, but she wasn't learning in a group environment. I kept thinking, if I look back on my life when I am eighty, will it matter more that I built a business or that I raised a child? I downsized my business from over four hundred to ten select clients and left my downtown office to work at home and study how to teach Liz. We set a homeschool start date eighteen-months away on April Fool's Day, 1997. Liz's

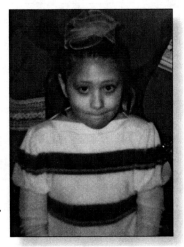

Please, please Mom. Let me come home—you teach me!" Yikes

job was to try her best during her remaining days in public school. My job was to get my finances in order, keep my select clients happy and learn how Liz learned to teach her.

Liz explained her school problems: *"Mom, it is like every year the teacher talks faster, and faster, and faster, and faster. I can't hear all the words. I can't remember. I have to make things up. I just answer whatever. I just check off boxes. I don't care if I get the wrong answer. I can't keep up. It makes me crazy. I hate my life."*

Years later she shared: *"Can you imagine Mom what it is like to know something one minute and have if disappear the next. Teachers didn't get it."*

Though she was committed to learn to read she placed her real energy into making friends. Once a child who avoided looking at people she now talked to every stranger on the street. From early attachment issues we thought we had come a long way. We invited her friends on bike rides for ice cream. We packed picnic lunches for excursions to the park and an older brother purchased a trampoline to increase Liz's gross motor skills, her balance and help her weight issue. Children filled our yard and Liz started a 'friend collection.' Even though she was hard on friendships, children kept coming. She never seemed to run out of young people she considered 'friends.'

Meanwhile, I researched how individuals process information—visual, auditory and kinesthetic. I discovered Liz acquired most of her information through hearing—and her hearing seemed to take in limited amounts of information at a time, miss pieces, and mix things up when outputting that information. I discovered I processed my information best visually. We were going to be some team—the deaf leading the blind.

Learning To ride a bike Was very hard.

I would throw it down and walk away.

When I finally learned to ride I flew over the handle bars when I wasn't looking. I don't know how. and I got hit by a car when a bag got in my wheels and the car didn't stop. My friend Mikey helped me up.

I didn't See The car. I still don't watch So well. I have a hard time paying attention

Liz's feet, hands and mind seemed to play a game of charades with her and would get all mixed up.

- **She had difficulty moving in different directions or up and down.**

In addition,

- **She was unable to cross either midline— horizontal or vertical.**

It would be years before we'd discover that Liz was living with mixed dominance and what that meant to her abilities, emotions and understanding.

Each of us acquires slightly different neurodevelopmental patterns. Many children and adults who experience difficulties in learning, task performance, or social interaction have neurodevelopmental differences which interfere with processing. For example, when the systems that support vision or the sense of position in space, are not strong enough, then reading, math, general organization and efficiency may suffer. Trauma may further complicate matters.

Judith Bluestone—www.handle.org

——

I finally understood mixed dominance when I stepped off with the wrong foot while bowling and didn't let go of the ball. I landed face down, ten feet into the alley, my ball finally free of my fingers. I in the gutter.

Jodee—FASD Mom

——

FROM LIZ ——*It's the little things about FASD that trip you. For example one side of my bottom lip has limited muscle control and I never know when it will turn off. If I am eating I drip food. If I am talking I may spit.*

Liz struggled so hard to overcome her coordination issues and she carefully hid years of hurtful comments she received regarding her clumsiness, inability to skip, her funny hop, run and jumping jacks. My heart broke watching her struggle to be like her peers—to rollerblade, skate, ski, jump on the trampoline and ride a bike. It would be years before I truly learned how to help Liz with balance, coordination and attention issues.(*Our FAScinating Journey- Keys to Brain Potential Along the Path of Prenatal Brain Injury*) Even though hearing was how she learned, I didn't know how her auditory processing deficits were affecting many parts of her life. If only I had known then what I know now.

While Liz focused on friends and activities. I focused on understanding Gardner's Eight Intelligences and teaching strategies. I wanted to be armed with as many strategies to teach material as possible. I knew Liz could learn, I just had to get the information creatively inside her brain and allow it to be retrieved. **To learn Liz had to think it was fun!**

GARDNER'S EIGHT INTELLIGENCES*

Musical/Rhythmic	Rhythm, music, melody. Incorporate music daily, tape record for listening, singing, recording, utilize rhythm and instrumentation.
Mathematical/Logical	Categorize, classify, work on patterns and relationships. Utilize manipulatives, games like checkers and chess, simple machines.
Body/Kinesthetic	Touch, move, interact. Physical challenges, spelling and grammar with dance, math with manipulatives, allow movement and interaction.
Spatial/Visual	Visualize, colors/pictures, map, draw, chart, diagram, puzzles
Linguistic/Verbal	Saying, hearing and seeing words. Listen, appreciate, reading aloud, spelling games, rhymes, tongue twisters, writing.
Natural	Explore, observe, collect, order. Explore outdoors, seek patterns and order within the world, collections, plants, animals
Interpersonal	Share, relate, cooperate, games that problem solve to figure out the knowledge or intent of another, discussion about social interactions.
Intrapersonal	Self-paced, individual, work alone. Express emotions, preferences, strategies, understand wishes, fears and how to cope, cozy quiet spaces.
	*Existential intelligence is under consideration

Armed with processing and intelligence knowledge, I still wasn't sure where to begin. Liz had become adept at faking what she didn't know and I was rapidly discovering there were many missing bricks in her education foundation. The other barrier I seemed to face was I never knew when her brain circuitry would shut down, misfire, or refire and sadly, neither did she.

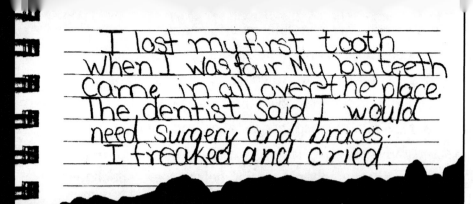

I lost my first tooth when I was four. My big teeth came in all over the place. The dentist said I would need surgery and braces. I freaked and cried.

Dental and medical experiences for children with FASD can be very traumatic, not just for the child, but for the parents who are providing support and comfort, and the professionals who are providing care.

Alert professional providers verbally and in writing of any unusual behaviors or reactions the child has previously exhibited.

- **Caution must be used in selecting anesthesia, medications and treatments.**
- **All medications the child is on must be reported to the professionals. Include all vitamins or supplements.**
- **Prepare the professional for your child, even if they think you are exaggerating.**

For your child, teen or adult we find that role play before you go with your child, teen or adult.

Watch your child carefully and document any changes the could be due to medication.

Professionals will need to be able to adapt their methods for the child's sake. While other children began to tolerate being able to wait for things, handle frustration or deal with disappointments children with FASD continue to struggle regulating their nervous systems as well as their emotions. Huge emotional responses can result from discontentment about anything.

When a change (transition) has occurred, the events of an outing are not within the scope of my son's thinking. He lives in the present. He may however recall them the next day, week, or month.

Vicki, FASD mom

———

FROM LIZ —*My world exists in NOW time. That means when I am doing something I keep doing it. I finish the process. If I am interrupted or plans change I have a very difficult time stepping into the next thing. The past is gone and I cannot see the future.*

ORAL LEARNING

Even at ages nine and ten, much of Liz's learning continued through oral stimulation. We were constantly dealing with wet sleeves, shirts, chairs, money and whatever else was handy to put into her mouth to help her better understand her world. She still had sucking issues and found unique methods of oral stimulation. She was a chatterbox. What ever thought popped into her mind flowed out her mouth. It seemed her mouth hadn't had a rest in ten years, except when she was sleeping and even then it sometimes enjoyed a dream-filled conversation. At least, we knew what she was thinking. Later in her teens, Liz announced she was hearing voices in her head. With questioning, we discovered her internal voice had emerged and she now was able think inside her head without having to hear herself say it. In some cases, silence is not always golden for parents.

One day as I registered for an appointment at the doctor's office, Liz's toddler nose went up in a twitter. She smelled something—most likely the antiseptic smell of a clinical environment. Off she ran, tongue protruding against the clinic's wall, tasting thirty feet of paint and germs. Horrified, I rushed to scoop up the little bundle of energy who now understood why the clinic smelled the way it did.

Another time when Liz was five, the dentist asked her to open her mouth and show him her beautiful teeth. The chocolate-smelling Magic Marker had been well sucked on in the waiting room and a mouthful of brown, discolored teeth glared at him.

As a toddler, Liz was Ms. Biter Extraordinaire. Instead of a kiss, I could expect a bite. She'd chomp onto my chin and hang on as I pried her off. Our home was filled with apples and carrots that we handed to her and said *"People bite food."*

Once Liz picked up Dr. Sagey Puddy Cat, the magical 'very much alive' cat, and took a chomp on his back. Worried for her safety, I picked her up and gave her a swat on the diaper saying *"Do not bite animals."* She'd never experienced that reaction and was quite shocked. In perfect FASD style, she turned, bit me and did not let go. Realizing this could go on for a long time, I said firmly *"Do not bite people."* I pried her off and put my hands lovingly on her little face looking eye to eye. *"No biting animals. No biting people,"* I reinforced. As I let go, she bit herself. Exasperated I said, *"Fine, bite yourself."*

We learn from our mistakes. First knowledge is vitally important for our neurologically impaired children. What we say is important. I wish someone had told me that all I needed to say was *"People bite food." "People eat food."* and *"People taste food."* Even as a teen, Liz struggled with biting herself when she was frustrated, scared, angry or in a rage. I wished so often I could retract those three little words. Time does not heal something, you have to correct it. **If you made a mistake—fix it now.**

Mom asked if there was anything else we could do. The dentist smiled and said pray. So we prayed for Three years.

That dentist died and The new dentist saw all pictures. She was sure to make money on my mouth.

But when I openned my Mouth my teeth were perfect. She asked me who fixed your teeth. I told her Jesus. She couldn't believe it.

We found out even minor surgeries in the hospital with our son need anesthesia. The doctors now insist that we stay in the room wearing surgical clothes. The last time my son fought the 'gas' mask with such force the doctors asked me to coax him and put the mask on him. I succeeded. I also succeeded in inhaling enough of the gas so I began to pass out. The next time we had a dental check-up, my son had no cavities. I overheard the dentist say, "Thank God!"

Susan, FASD mom

___

Children with FASD seem to be constantly on the go, never settling down or satisfied. They will move from activity to activity never really focusing. They may engage in the same type of movement over and over again.

___

FROM LIZ —I don't do sarcasm. What you say to me is what I hear—exactly what the words mean. If you tell me to do something I will do it. If you tease me with sarcasm I will not know you are fooling around, I will be wounded by your words and mean spirit.

Dental and medical visits provide two things our children with FASD have great difficulty with: over stimulation and transition

1. **Over stimulation due to the lights, sounds, smells, new people, and necessary procedures.**
2. **Transition from the house, to the car, to the waiting room, to the examination room. By exam time we are already down four changes.**

They get on an emotional roller coaster— confused, stuck, overwhelmed, fear, anxious, rageful. Stay grounded yourself you do not have to join them.

DENTAL ISSUES

We are attentive to dental hygiene. Our baby's teethe on a soft toothbrush. It's a personal care priority, but tactile defensive children may avoid brushing. We discovered Liz cooperated as long as we did not invade her personal space and made things fun and interesting.

Chillin' with my toothbrush

Liz, age one, enjoyed sitting on the bathroom counter, her little feet in the sink, as we brushed our teeth. She chewed a little toothbrush a tiny drop of toothpaste. She watched us make funny faces, laugh and spit in the sink. We rolled our eyes, stuck out our tongues and winked at her. She copied us while standing on the counter, watching herself brush her teeth and make funny faces. Rearing a child to raise an adult—takes repeatable very tiny steps to establish lifetime patterns.

Liz, age three, joined me on my dental visits. Our dentist let her sit on my lap and watch. He'd peek in her mouth as he did my dental work. He praised her as a great dental assistant while she stood on a little stool and held the vacuum to evacuate my saliva. She loved squirting Mom's mouth with the water hose and hit my face with a missed burst. He let her push the x-ray button. She and the dentist looked at the pictures to decide what to do with Mom. By letting her participate in dentistry, he captured her attention and cooperation. Our normally fearful, raging child developed a fond relationship with our dentist and he was able to work with her because of this relationship.

Looking back, I should have realized something was unusual when she lost her two front teeth at age four and had the front adult teeth at age five. By age six, Liz had most of her permanent teeth. She lost her final baby tooth at eight. By age nine, she had reached her full adult stature—a very large nine-year-old who is now a very petite adult.

Her new teeth were in disarray, jutting here and there within her mouth. Her lower jaw was offset from her upper jaw, her mouth unable to close. Our dentist was very concerned and felt we'd soon need ENT intervention.

Liz exploded into a FASD dental chair meltdown, as she heard him discuss tooth pulling , orthodontia, and surgery that was to come. I asked if there were any other alternatives. He smiled and laughingly said, "Well, I guess you can pray."

Once Liz gets an idea into her head she is immovable and she prayed faithfully every night for three years. Today, her teeth remain straight and her jaw is aligned. For Liz, what is said, is what it is or will be. In this case, the sarcastic remark worked instead of hurt. She developed her personal faith based relationship and pray life. Praise the Lord!

I got a womans body really early too, I was only 8 when I would steel moms packing tape and wrap my chest so no one would know I wouldn't let any one see me.

The boys would say"did you stuff your bra today" or "you're a big butt!" It was hard to have a 16 year old body and be a little girl.

I just wanted to get out of School so bad and I would beg mom to home school me.

Living as a concrete learner in an abstract world is complicated. Rarely, do people who think in abstraction say exactly what they mean and this becomes a dangerous slope for the person with FASD. Most preteens begin abstract reasoning, enter middle school, seek independence and struggle with identity. Because the teen with FASD experiences the world different from the accepted norm, he compares himself to the status quo.

What results may be a poor sense of self, gravitation to peers who use the person with FASD for their dirty work and self soothing strategies with drugs, alcohol or sex.

There is am emotional and mental difference in puberty when your world remains in concrete operations, rather than abstraction.

Children with FASD start falling behind more noticeably around the fourth grade. There is an increase in the demands of verbal competence, reliance on reading, and emphasis on abstract thought. The child feels abandoned and isolated. Holding on to the pieces of understanding they seem sure of they may become inflexible, rigid and set in their ways. It is a common season of lashing our and may include attacks the very people who are coming to save them—much like a person drowning.

In addition, on some level, the child may feel at fault for not being able to learn or achieve. Anger is a normal feeling. It is the choices we sometimes make when we're angry that may not be good. As the parent of a child with FASD, I get angry too. Angry at the overt reactions, at the frustration, at the anger— angry all this was preventable.

Jodee, FASD mom

PRECOCIOUS PUBERTY

After Liz lost her two front teeth, at four, she began to gain weight and grow taller. We were encouraged because she had always been teeny tiny. Looking back, I now understand that the weight gain was the beginning of her changes toward womanhood. If I had known we could have been prepared to help her instead of frustrate her.

When Liz was seven she informed me she could take care of herself and I didn't need to help her bathe or dress. She needed her privacy, and her teacher said no one should see her body except the doctor. We told her if she could manage her hygiene we'd agree, but if she let herself be dirty or not care for her body, we'd intervene. She continued to manage good hygiene and we respected her privacy. Then suddenly our home office packing tape disappeared. Little did we know our eight-year-old was carefully wrapping her chest so no one knew she had breasts and that she stealthily camouflaged her development with careful hygiene. She reached her adult stature of 5'1" at age nine and experienced first menses at age eight. And we thought it was a childhood growth spurt! It was the beginning of hiding the reality of her personhood.

We never guessed our little girl was stealing her 17 year-old sister's sanitary protection for her own use and that she was too scared to tell us about the sexual statements made by boys who teased and called her names. Since we'd told her she was not allowed to use those words— she didn't think she had permission to say them. She continued to gain weight and get more sullen and surly.

Finally, Liz came home for school. Her life felt safe, simple and secure. Within the first months of homeschool, she ate well and lost 17 pounds. She was smiling. She was ready for summer. We laughed again. Homeschooling removed the stress from her life. She no longer compare herself with other children. I was there to answer questions and provide support. We had hours of one-on-one time, and we focused on playful learning, nutrition, health and self-esteem. She loved her trampoline and gained coordination and balance—as we jumped through spelling and math drills—which helped her maintain focus.

Home school with Mom,
I was finally home and safe.

Precocious or late puberty is common for children with FASD. For the lucky children who develop late—the world allows them more room for their childish behaviors. For children like Liz, who was one of the smallest preschool children and a fully developed woman by age nine—the world is not kind.

When I got angry I used to scratch myself, bite myself, band my head and pull my hair out. Now I know that hurting myself doesn't really help the anger even if it stopped it. I told mom it didn't hurt when I did those things, but the next day it would hurt or I would have a black and blue marks.

When I get angry now I go to my mom or pray or bite paper. They help me settle down.

What to do?

"REMAIN CALM"

- Keep the person safe.
- Limit the number of new situations.
- Know your child. Read the danger signals.
- Avoid overstimulating activities.
- Teach and practice appropriate responses to overstimulating activities.
- Avoid prolonged periods of desk work.
- Provide short breaks.
- Keep tasks simple, teach with baby steps.
- Don't judge the person for a rage.
- Love the child unconditionally.
- Model mature and safe authority.

Over stimulation SAFE plan

S - Scan area for sensory overload points

A - Ask yourself —are there issues that can become overwhelming

F - Give freedom to leave when needed

E - Exit (see ideas page ---)

———

"Mom, I have hitters, biters and kickers and screamers inside of me. I need to get them out," Liz shrieked. Together we lay on the floor kicking, yelling and banging our fists. Liz rolled over and hugged me saying, "Mom, we forgot the biters. I think we can save them for another day."

———

Limbic rage victims frequently kick, spit, gouge, claw, and use obscene language. It is often marked by great strength and speed, making escape difficult. In many, a vestige of self-control remains. This may take the form of diverting the rage away from others onto inanimate objects or the self. Limbic rage is very disruptive to the people who have it and to the people in their environment.

Virginia Scott —The Brain, Fact, Function, Fantasy

BRAIN 'STORMS' - RAGES TO RUN PARENTS RAGGED

For years Liz had incredible rages that lasted from fifteen minutes to two hours. Her body tensed and her face turned fearful as she threw herself on the floor growling, snarling and screaming. A medical exam showed nothing was wrong. We had learned from experience intervention only escalated and prolonged the tirade, so we remained calm and carefully monitored her safety until she got up and walked away as if nothing happened. Public rages were embarrassing as eyes and scowls of judgment scanned our daughter and our parenting ability. Standing in long lines, crowded spaces or unstructured environments like fairs or auditoriums flipped an invisible switch to an electrical 'brainstorm' that quickly escalated. It was frightening and exhausting to watch! Karl and I focused on maintaining our emotional health. We didn't enhance her chaos—she needed order to trust control.

I told her, "Your rages scare me and I don't know what to do when they happen. Do you have any ideas?"

Liz explained, "Mom, I don't know what it is. It's like energy in my toes. Then it goes up my ankles and my legs into the knees. After that I have no control—I can't stop myself."

"Wow!" I said, "I think we need a fire drill to stop it as soon as it hits your toes. Let's think of ways to catch this energy." We decided that she'd say, "Mom, I need help," and I'd put my hands on her shoulders and look her directly in the eyes and say, "Liz, I love you. You're a really good kid. You are special to God, your family and many others." She repeated back my statements until she returned words of "I love me, I am a good kid, or I am okay." Sometimes I didn't believe her calls for help, or stop to take the time she needed and she'd fall enraged to the floor until her neurological thunderstorm blew over. Then when the sun shone again from her eyes and her rainbow smile emerged she'd ask, "Mom, why didn't you help me?" My heart broke many times. We grew together and within two months, Liz began talking herself out of the anger before they became infantile rages. We managed Liz's environment as much as possible and watched for the danger signs. Most of all we didn't judge the brainstorms. We loved the child.

LIZ SHARES, I still struggle everyday with anger issues. It is almost like a constant job to fight all the pieces of misinformation that comes against me, sort it out and understand the reality. That process can be overwhelming and if someone is accusing me of something I did not do, calling a mistake in public, or being demeaning I can still get mad too quickly. That means I act out or say things I wish I could take back. Somehow, Sam and I will figure out how to over come these grizzly mind bears—we are starting with **"Heart Smart Steps"**.

I used lie alot. The words would just fall out of my mouth, then I felt bad and wondered why I said that. I still lie sometimes, but not to my family. Most I lie to be like other kids.

When I was 12 I tried everything, drugs cigarettes, alcohol sex and other stuff.

I wanted to be like everyone else. Mom and dad found out and helped me understand why all those.

I believed every one was doing it too.

One day I realized that my child was the cameraman in his life experiences and that was why he never "did" the things I or other people saw him do.

Ann Yurcek, author, Tiny Titan Journey of Hope

Two way communication means that both people understand clearly what the other is trying to say. When I speak a foreign language I sound skilled if I am the only one doing the talking, but please don't ask me difficult questions or try to have a conversation.

For my daughter, social events are her number one trigger. Going anywhere put us at risk of a meltdown. She didn't know what to do, she is triggered by sensory stimuli either at the event or from the anxiety to attend the event. We have to role play the event and prompt each step of the way—and if we don't keep practicing some small event everyday we loose what we've gained.

1. *Pre-prime to make room for her brain to have space to accept what you are telling her and help her accept what is going to happen.*
2. *Then wait and repeat without overwhelming her.*
3. *The night before we warn her we are going*
4. *Prepare her to go—step by step—often repeating each step twice.*
5. *Prompt each step so she knows what to do.*
6. *Celebrate the steps*
7. *Reprocess and enjoy the telling of the day.*

Ann Yurcek, author, FASD
Mom to 7, Tiny Titan

THE VALUE OF TRUTH

The virtue of truth is a cornerstone in our foundation. As foster parents, we learned that the children we cared for often had great difficulty with truth telling and so we developed the Truth Counsel table. A Truth Counsel could be called by any family member guilty of any offense as an easy way out of any problem. Truth before being caught by a parent equalled Freedom and Forgiveness. If the guilty person called the counsel and the discussion surrounding the issue was sincere, we granted redemption. If there was an offense done against another, the person presenting the case suggested the restitution to be made and got agreement from person offended.

Once, at age four, Liz announced she was calling a Truth Counsel right this minute! Karl and I took our chairs as Liz crawled up and stood on my chair hiding behind my back. Karl asked her to state her issue. She explained she had toileting problems and messes in her pants.

"Well, what are you going to do about it?" my husband asked.

"I'm going to go to the bathroom right this minute!" she hopped off the chair for the first of bathroom visits every five to fifteen minutes. Our plumbing inspector had emerged to become a nightmare for schools and other programs.

We carefully monitored television, computer and videogames. We drew a hard line between pretend (which Liz doesn't understand very well) and reality. Santa Claus, Tooth Fairy and Easter Bunny were relegated to the same status as an actor playing dress-up. Pretend meant we used our minds for a short time to solve a problem, we didn't use it to fool or trick people.

I separate deliberate lying, manipulation or sneakiness—which a person does to remain safe or to hide an action or behavior, and blurting—when words and actions occur as the first thing the person could think of or do. I liken her tales and descriptions to a power surge while I am writing a computer file, the input, never matches the output.

We have been shocked many times with the incredible tall tales flowing fluidly from the mouth of someone who seems to have a limited imagination. We listen carefully to discover what she is trying to say, playing the sleuth by separating and rearranging the patched words to develop the reality. We find her stories mixed with real life or television experiences and her reality of an event seldom matched ours as she can rarely see herself in the picture.

Over time we have learned that Liz's experiences in the world are different from ours because of her sensory, body and brain differences. Little things we overlook she may magnify. Large things that we believe matter she may shut out.

Finally mom let me come home when I was 10 years old.

I learned much easier it was just me and mom. She threw the alphabet out the door, and slammed it shut and we started at the vary beinning. learning in vary little steps. Mom didn't teach me new things until I knew the old things.

I felt safe with mom.

We study all the things other kids study. We go on trips and we cook and make things.

I don't get a frusteated when I learn in tiny steps.

I work primarily with at-risk students. I must rebuild them from the foundations. After six or seven years of failure with our language, they have little or no confidence and less self-esteem. Handwriting is the first area where students believe in themselves again.

Success begets success.

- Jay Patterson, author
Reading Works & Grammar Works

While turning onto a icy winter road, I slid across the center lane into bright orange cones. The cones flew high into the air and Liz exclaimed, "Now, do you know how I feel when I cross my midline!"

———

Liz puts forth great effort to learn and remember. Yet, the next day her brain's filing system locks the drawers. School becomes a never ending nightmare.

———

Excerpt: "F is for Finding Hope"
"I am not able to tell you what I'm thinking, but I will find a way. I don't understand all your words, but I will do my best to do what you ask.

I am not able to move in the direction you want me too, but I will move. My brain skips. It short circuits. It misses. It does not connect. I may not know how to please you, but I'm trying! The more I try to understand and do, sometimes, the more confused I get. The more I try to please you, the more I mess up."

Ann Kagarise, FASD Life Expert, photographer, blogger:
livingwithfasd.wordpress.com

SAFE AT HOME BASE

Even with special school services reading continued to pose a major problem for Liz. A friend, who had been homeschooling her child with reading difficulties, told me about *The Writing Road to Reading* by Romalda Spalding. She invited me to attend a week-long training course for teachers scheduled for the summer before I began homeschooling. The teacher, Jay Patterson, consistently achieved two to five year advances in reading with his students and he had stomped through the pitfalls of teaching reading to hundreds of students with difficulties. I signed up, hoping to discover ideas to teach Liz.

Homeschooling gave me the freedom to try new looks.

Jay's adventure began when his nine-year-old son could not spell, even though he read and spoke English fluently. Jay tried to apply his years of classroom experience with his conventional wisdom. It did not work. He searched and found a program that surpassed his expectations. In over ten years, it has not let his students down.

The first day of his training program, Jay shared an essay by Shari Anderson, titled *"Why I Like Spalding Manuscript."* The handwriting was beautiful. The essay, he went on, was written by a student in his English class after two years of rebuilding and reintroducing basic concepts and principles of our language. As he showed the paper a teacher in the front row began crying. Jay knew little about this child's history except that she arrived at his class with little confidence and was plagued by previous academic failure. The school file labeled her MMMI—mild to moderately mentally impaired.

The teacher went on to explain why she was crying. *"Shari was in my fifth grade class. Elementary school was very difficult for her and she chose to do nothing. She would sit and that's about it. She had experienced so much failure in those early years she was afraid of risking success. No confidence. Lots of fear. No desire to risk more hurt. No willingness to try."*

The teacher was both incredulous and overjoyed at Shari's progress. She saw this composition as a miracle. My heart soared with hope. Nothing anyone had tried so far worked for Liz in writing, reading or spelling.

Jay Patterson captured my full attention. *"Metalinguistics is a process that transcends the empowering nature of multi-sensory instruction and the four avenues to the brain,"* Jay began.

We needed empowerment.

Four avenues to the brain—which one did I miss?

When I get into a problem it is hard for me to get out of the problem. I don't know how I got there and I don't know what to do. Then I freak or yell or say stuff I don't mean. I used to get really angry and lay on the floor and growl. I learned to get angry at the anger getting rone.

I also learned that eating good food, sleeping right and vitamins helped turn my special life into good.

Teaching in a multi-sensory way means that we must involve the student

1. Hear it — Auditory
2. See it — Visual
3. Do it — Kinesthetic
4. Say It — Vocal

"Tell me and I'll forget;
show me and I may remember;
involve me and I'll understand."

Chinese Proverb

Shared by Rob Wybretch FASD Life Expert

Every time you see a smidgen of success, you dance in the aisles or on the kitchen table and you celebrate because they have won the biggest game in town. Don't mind the neighbors. Just dance.

——

As an instructor you keep telling students they are sharp, that their self-discipline and their focusing on details is out of sight. I tell them that they need this precise neurological record to become better readers, writers and spellers. Building dependability, responsibility, and accountability for handling language with care can begin when students are expected to handle something as simple and foundational as the correct formation of letters and letter placement.

Jay Patterson (1999)

——

"Most obstacles melt away when we make up our minds to walk boldly through them"
Orison Swett Marden

Quote shared by Chanel Torres.
FASD Life Expert, co-author,
With Heavy Hand and Heart,
:Love Mommy

MOM EVICTS THE ALPHABET

Students learn by what they hear from others, what they see, what they do with their hands and what they personally say from their mouths. These are the four avenues to the brain: visual, auditory, kinesthetic and vocal. I realized Liz learned vocally—the one avenue no one had been letting her use. I immersed myself in Jay's class to learn everything I could. We started at the very beginning.

Dr. Samuel Torrey Orton (1878-1948) a well-known neuropathologist, spent his career researching how the brain best learns language. His passion became researching the reasons why certain students were dyslexic and unable to read or write. From his meticulous studies emerged the well-known Orton-Gillingham and Slingerland programs and the text *The Writing Road to Reading* by Romalda Spalding.

Liz needed to learn her way around a sheet of paper. We began our first lessons in manuscript writing. She learned the page points, short lines, long lines, circles, portions of circles, the clock points and their respective legal definitions. She learned how to hold a pencil, how to sit and how to look at the paper. She learned where to place the paper and keep your head. And then Mom did the unthinkable. In a grand swoop she picked up the dastardly alphabet and threw him out the door.

Liz locked the door laughing hysterically. I had captured her attention and she smiled. I had her curiosity and the beginning of trust, because I understood her pain. We were going to rewire neurons and build her attentional capacity. I had captured her commitment to try. So much for day one. Now homeschool would provide a safe harbor for Liz to repair her broken academic sails.

As we worked with the Spalding method I came to realize that the difference between the names of the alphabet characters and the sounds of their phonemes was too great a leap for Liz. What seemed like simple instruction for others was an insurmountable mountain climb for her. Though she could sing the alphabet song, she was unable to match letters to the multitude of confusing sounds. She had learned to watch others carefully and mimic, but she truly did not understand. I was often astounded at her creativity to mask what she could not grasp so her teachers believed she was learning. I felt honored to be given her truth and trust and be allowed to teach her.

Liz needed success at handling language at the most elementary level with phonograms (sound pictures), the knowledge that certain letters and combinations of letters make certain sounds in a word. These phonograms became the tiny building blocks to a solid core understanding of reading, writing and spelling. Orton's remarkable neurological research gave us a bridge. Liz had detoured the alphabet attack and come home.

Things were bad for me.
Now I am Tering not to do any of them and proud of it to. I even help the little kids not get into all that stuff.

Their mom's mom's say I am an good example. But my friend tasha's mom says I'm a ho.

Frustration Alert & Stop Program.

1. **STEP BACK and STOP !**
2. **BREATHE. Relax your body and breathe deeply through your nose into your heart and smile "I can do it".**
3. **BREAKDOWN the behavior into smaller parts with each breath.**
   a. **What's my problem?**
   b. **What am I doing?**
   c. **Where am I?**
   d. **Who is affected?**
   e. **How can I change?**
4. **Brainstorm ideas to CHANGE.**

HAVE FUN!   Live - Laugh - Love!
Chill out - Failure is an opportunity to learn a new way to do something.

Discipline is different from punishment because it teaches children to learn from their mistakes instead of fear and suffer for them. It provides the next step for growth. I think discipline should be immediate and tied directly and tangibly to the reason for the discipline. Discipline that is abstract, deferred, or requires memory, reason, reflection and foresight may not work well.

Bob Schacht, Ph.D.

——

Refusing to discipline a child because you believe they cannot help their behavior sets them up for failure and you up for unnecessary struggles.

Lori, FASD mom

——

1. FASD is a lifetime body and brain difference.
2. When a person feels safe, trusts you and enjoys being in your presence you will get the most learning
3. You are rearing a child but raising an adult
4. Living in a world of concrete operations as an adult is a brilliant and wonderful place that most adults forget to enjoy because their brains have moved to abstraction.

FROZEN FRUSTRATION BALLS

David rejoined our family as a homeschool exchange student. Diagnosed with FAS he challenged his mother, his school and his family. We'd made progress with Liz in home-school. Could we also school and care for Dave?

No one understands why kids like Dave act the way they do. It is easy to point fingers and assign blame. Dave looks normal and can function normally, at least for a while. FASD behavior is not due to inadequate parenting and many healthy and skilled families care for children with FASD and the complex behaviors caused by the child's brain injuries and metabolic difference can confound anyone.

One day, reaching my own sensory overload—overwhelmed with not being able to teach, tired of Liz and Dave's self abusing behavior, frustrated with their frustration—I screamed and pulled out my hair. My reaction immediately stopped Dave and Liz and their mouths hung open and their eyes wide. In unison they said *"Mom, are you OK?"*

"No, I was not OK. I was demonstrating their behavior back to them like a mirror." We spent the rest of the school day setting new strategies.

Dave said, *"Mom you say, you can get mad but you never hurt people. Why did you hurt yourself?"*

And I said, *"Good question,'why' questions are the hard ones to answer. Let's figure it out."* We came up with things we could do to let our steam out and not hurt ourselves. Asking for help became top priority with praise and prizes for not exploding.

Dave, who was eight, made a 'frustration ball' with crumpled paper surrounded by happy yellow tape. He placed it in the freezer to keep it frozen so the frustration couldn't seep out and get him. When he felt frustrated, he took the ball out of the freezer, squished the frustration back into his ball, threw the ball back in the freezer, and slammed the door banning the frustration into a frozen jail.

Liz, then eleven, dictated a To Do list to take care of her frustrations: crush cans, crumple paper for the wood stove, take a hot bath with bubbles, watch myself be mad in the mirror, cuddle in my blanket, close my eyes and breath deep, jump rope, pull weeds, break sticks for fire, pump the player piano, play with clay, ride bike, go for a walk, dance, count to ten, clean the dog kennel. Yuck!

We shared these acceptable outlets for the children's frustration with our professional support people, friends and family members. Mom made up her own plan. I gave myself permission to go to my room for time out and Dave and Liz promised to leave me alone for a five minute vacation and not knock on the door or yell. "Mom!"

I needed to learn to care for me!

My mom and sent me to a therapist. She annoyed me and got into my business.

She made me really mad. I hated seeing her. She didn't understand me. She sent me to a psychiatrist who said I have FAS. At first I was mad. Now I know I am not responsible for getting it but I have to learn to live with it.

Nothing was making sense. Our daughter was an obedient child. She desired to be good. She wanted to please. Yet, it felt as though she was deliberately sabotaging every effort we made to provide her love and care.

When we fail to recognize a person with FASD we set up the client and ourselves for weeks, months or years of one frustrating treatment failure after another... When the underlying disability of FASD is recognized, it provides a point of reference for appropriate intervention.

Kenneth Dunning, FASD dad

The fetal alcohol diagnosis made sense. We finally reached the core issue. Now that we knew what was wrong, what could be done?

———

I love doing the work of FASD, we have so many youth who live outside of the box and their ideas are awesome. I share my view of things and they share their view of things, then we sit back and say, "Wow, we think alike, oh that's because we both live with FASD and we live outside of the box!" We laugh and enjoy conversations, we cry when times are tough, we share and swap stories of struggles and good times. I love being FASD even when its tough and I am on an express way of learning.

James Gideon, FASD Life Expert Coach/Trainer, Program Coordinator: Enhanced Extrajudicial Sanctions Program (Diversion Program), Equine Assisted Life Skills Training,

———

Liz struggled with Brain Gym® and cross tapping exercises because even at 14 she had not mastered crossing her midline.

THERAPY OPENED DOORS

As soon as we discovered Liz was experimenting with high risk adolescent behaviors, we sought a qualified therapist. We were getting in over our heads—rages, learning disabilities, attachment and adoption issues, anger, resentment, lies, thefts we were managing. But adding sex, cigarettes, alcohol and marijuana all within seventeen days of turning twelve we were up to our necks in quicksand!

Therapy provided us a framework to help Liz. Each week her counselor provided homework on a targeted issue. Since it was therapist focused instead of parent focused, the negative emotions were directed at the therapist rather than us. Liz's therapist empowered us to support and encourage our daughter as she worked her way through fear, hurt, inadequacy, anger and frustration. We opened doors on adoption issues, peer pressure, and sexuality. We worked as a team to help Liz deal with issues of impulsivity, anger and frustration. Still it seemed talk therapy was not enough, what else could we do?

Running late for therapy one day, I dropped Liz off and rushed over to the golden arches to fill her order of two cheeseburgers, fries and a soda. Liz had been calm before I delivered her lunch. She ate it while her therapy session continued and soon after began shouting, jumping, screaming and using four-letter words with the therapist. Food was our only difference. The therapist contributed no other triggers. Could diet be causing some of our significant behaviors? I made an appointment with a clinical nutritionist while the therapist referred us to a well-respected psychiatrist for an evaluation and diagnosis.

The psychiatrist noted that Liz's history glared with the details of fetal alcohol exposure. FASD had been there all the time, but no one put the pieces together. Her behaviors were symptoms of neurological brain damage. Pieces of our puzzle started joining. The diagnosis was a bittersweet gift. Karl and I alone know Liz as a whole person—24/7, 365 days a year and love her unconditionally just because she exists. We know her in many situations with many combinations of life experiences. I realized professionals each understood separate pieces of our child. So armed with a diagnosis, we sought the best individuals in FASD, traumatic brain injury and learning disabilities. We searched for medical doctors, occupational therapists, physical therapists, teachers, nutritionists and/or neurodevelopmentalists to help us. It would be our job to determine the path to follow in taking counsel from those who had walked this way before us. **But what path?**
Each person with FASD is affected differently.

We added FASD to our list of medical diagnosis. This piece fit and made sense. We now knew what. Now how to help?

We found a doctor who helped me learn how my body works and what to eat to keep me healthy and not have headaches. Before I would have headaches every day.

Now it happens only sometimes and they are not as bad.

I can't eat wheat or corn syrup or caffeine or MSG at all. At first I thought that was the end of my world.

Now we found other solutions and made up recipes that really taste good. I also lost 37 pounds and I look pretty.

Some Best Brain Foods

- **Salmon**
- **Turkey**
- **Vegetables**
- **Spinach**
- **Swiss Chard**
- **Collard Greens**
- **Bananas**
- **Orange Juice**
- **Blueberries**
- **Concord Grape Juice**
- **Milk**
- **Hot Cocoa**
- **Whole Grains**
- **Brown Rice**
- **Almonds/Walnuts**
- **Olive Oil**
- **Garlic**

. . . As research unveils the complex biochemistry of the human brain and the intimate connection between what we eat and what we create, this knowledge can enable us to function at our best.

———

Brain nutrition has four primary aspects, each corresponding to a class of food. Like the sides of a pyramid, they work together to create, protect, power and activate your brain.

1. *Structure - Fats for essential fatty acids and cell membrane integrity.*
2. *Protection - Fruits and vegetables for antioxidants and brain cell longevity.*
3. *Energy - Carbohydrates for glucose and energy production.*
4. *Function - Proteins for amino acids and neurotransmitter synthesis.*

Basically you need fatty acids to build your brain, antioxidants to safeguard it, glucose to fuel it, and amino acids to interconnect it . . .

MacArthur—Nutrition & Your Brain

CLEANING THE CUPBOARDS

Liz and I arrived at the clinical nutritionist's office a bit early. Per her usual waiting room behavior, she sat, she stood, she paced, she talked loudly and rudely. Per my usual mothering behavior, I tried to manage her to little avail as we registered, filled out papers, and proceeded to talk with a health coach. The fluorescent lights gave her headaches. She didn't like meeting new people and adding a nutritionist to her repertoire of professionals was offensive.

Our nutritionist, Dr. Brist, had successful experience in working with people with Downs Syndrome, schizophrenia and alcoholism, but had never worked with fetal alcohol exposure. He assessed Liz to determine suspect foods for intolerance and gave us a list of foods to avoid for the next thirty days. I promised to find replacements for her favorite foods and over the next thirty days eliminate those suspected of causing her trouble. The doctor committed to research fetal alcohol exposure, nutrition and supplements. We joined forces to see what we could do.

Liz was overwhelmed and proceeded to hit the walls and melt down in his office. We celebrated the new diet change with our last fast food sandwich and soda. Then I returned alone two hours later for a private consultation to learn as much as I could to help my daughter.

My kitchen was going to need an overhaul—wheat, dairy, caffeine, MSG, sugar, preservatives, dyes and corn products were to be eliminated. At that period of time it seemed corn syrup and hydrogenated fats lived in everything. By the time I got done eliminating the stuff we couldn't, shouldn't and wouldn't eat for the test my cupboards were bare. By the time I restocked our kitchen my bank account was emptied. But the results were worth every penny and minute of this investment.

Liz was remarkably less frenetic and impulsive after a month of turning our family diet upside down. Our home was more peaceful than it had been in over twelve years. Her headaches were reduced by half.

Dr. Brist used clear language and remarkable compassion to tell Liz how her body worked and how the nutritional supplements he prescribed could help her body process food and thus help her brain. The psychiatrist assured us we could pull Liz off the supplements and replace them immediately with medication if they did not work.

That first week, Liz exclaimed, *"Mom, I can think!"* She proceeded to memorize 45 states and capitals, learn her multiplication, understand the concept of division and write a song. Unprecedented!

> I like helping my friends when they have problems. When I am sitting with them talking I come up with good ideas and I am really kind and considerate.
>
> I know what it feels like to have problems so I am sensitive to my friends when they hurt. I am a happy person My eyes Sparkle and mom Says I Shine!

Our daughter has such a passion for being like everyone else, without a clear understanding of who everyone else is. She chooses inappropriate role models and they become her standard of 'normal.' Keeping her safe is very difficult.

Our children with FASD struggle in a world that doesn't understand their issues caused from central nervous system damage. The very teens who have compassion for a person with visible impairments may avoid or tease teens with FASD because they think they are weird. This is not unusual since teens with FASD are very gullible and naive. They react impulsively without restraint. Authoritative intervention escalates their behavior. As other teens are developing abstract reasoning, our children with FASD remain locked in concrete operations.

This was not an issue that would disappear. The diagnosis gave me the understanding that I was dealing with brain injury and it was my job to step back, regroup and understand what to do next.

Karl - FASD Dad

——

Flying with Broken wings is my full time job! Generally 18 hours a day, as long as I'm close to a pc I'm here. I deliver pamphlets to medical offices for display, and work to set up a support group locally for those of us living with FASD. I also speak to and for people living with FASD, as well as try and translate to those who don't 'get it'. I have to admit that I only had the time to get into this after my spine was broken in two places due to an industrial accident. That gave me PLENTY of time to read and learn and now gives me the time to work on my favorite project ever…"Learning to FLY!" I think it was Our Creator's way of telling me I had something important to do…

R.J. Formanek, FASD Life Expert
Facebook Group
"Flying with Broken Wings"

I believe today, most of what happened to Liz that first week on nutritional supplements was retrieval of stored information unavailable to her access. In any case, this sudden surge in knowledge gave Liz a new boost of self-esteem.

Liz's stomach aches ceased, her dizziness disappeared, and her headaches lessened to one per week. Her behavior stabilized and we began enjoying Liz's special naive innocence and unusual outlook on life. She started to like herself and try new experiences without her normal negativity. She spoke to us, her eyes sparkled, and her voice was positive. Her weight melted off as she ate the those foods her body was able to process well. Teaching her became something I looked forward to. She experimented with new hairstyles and clothes, establishing her own identity.

Liz was able to manage herself within reason. She took ownership of her diet and supplement program. She let me know when she was running low so she did not run out. Her therapist observed her drastic improvement. Our weekly visits became bi-weekly, monthly and then no longer necessary. We had a child we could manage.

Could this have happened through diet and supplements alone? If so, did she need all of them? Could we return to some of her favorite foods? I devoured nutritional books.

Things were working. I wasn't interested in upsetting the apple cart (the apples seemed to just fall out of Liz's cart all on their own).

I volunteer with youth groups to keep an open perspective on my daughter's strengths, differences and challenges. Working with neurologically undamaged children provides me with the understanding of the areas where Liz needs additional support or remediation. Liz's Cadette Girl Scout Troop headed to the Black Hills, South Dakota for a week of camping—our menu loaded with soft white bread and lots of carbohydrates, incredible environmental changes, daily transitions, and group experiences. On the third day, Liz ran out of one of her five supplements. Fortunately, I was there as a troop leader and I assured her it probably would not make a difference. How wrong I was! Within the next twenty-four hours, she attacked me and drew blood, ran away, and reverted to her old behaviors—we had four days to go! Her impulsivity escalated alongside frustration and anger. It became vital that the Troop understand fetal alcohol brain damage, participate in the strategies for her success and provide support to help her regain control. This was the first time I had to expose Liz's prenatal brain and body injuries to the public—FASD and its realities. It was our first beginning step in advocacy.

We now knew:

1. *Memory problems led to her confabulation.*
2. *Frontal lobe problems led to lack of empathy or reading social cues.*
3. *Limbic system problems led to blind rages that surpass logic.*

We began providing literature on fetal alcohol exposure

Now that I am a teenager I like still being a kid and sometimes more adult.

I talk with my mom to learn new things, or when I am confused or worried.

She listens and help me understand without saying big words or a long conversation.

She shows me how to do things different, and we practice them so I know it in my heart and my head.

According to Diane Malbin persons working with individuals affected by FASD must try differently not harder. Authoritativeness, aloofness and coldness trigger negative behaviors. My confusion or frustration can magnify my daughter's reactions and place everyone at risk. Every social skill must be taught and retaught. Cause and affect must constantly be reinforced.

Fear can become dangerous.

Impulsivity without restraint can lead to jail or worse for our children with FASD. The young person often has a terrible time comprehending the limited freedom given to him by parents. Things may become volatile as the child strives for independence and the parent adds restrictions. There must be a balance between protection and freedom to keep him safe and prevent him from danger. FASD young people often deny the reality of being unable to make sound judgments.

Barb, FASD mom

———

Growing up, I was always in and out of psychiatric hospitals and was discharged without a clue of what was wrong with me. I would shoplift, steal and pull fire alarms. I was easily swayed to do the wrong thing.

Steve, FASD Life Expert

———

I want to be like everyone else. I want people to think I am special too. I am sorry I lie because then I have to pay the consequences. I don't like that.

Miko, FASD Life Expert, age 9

OUR ULTIMATE CONSEQUENCE

FASD does not give a person the license to harm themselves, other people, animals or property. The circumstances of camping bombarding Liz, increasing her hidden fears and anxiety did not excuse violence. My husband and I drew our line in the sand. As an adult she could be jailed and/or fined—her life was already too complicated to include a future criminal record. Society considers her offense assault, her camp behavior qualified as disorderly conduct. We told Liz there would be a Truth Counsel in two days. She was to think about her offense and prepare for a Trial, because 'we the parents' arrested her for physically harming a person. She'd appear in front of judge Dad. During school, I prepared the defendant. We discussed court systems, legal words, and what happens to people who cause harm to others. We discussed what 'under oath' meant and what happens in court if you don't tell the truth. At our mock trial, Liz presented her case. She was forthright and honest.

"There were extenuating circumstances. I ran out of my nutrients. I was in a strange place. The food was bad for me." Liz was right she had been dealing with many transitions and changes—the legal world would not care about the 'how come' just the 'outcome'.

Mom presented her side, *"I had asked Liz to get out of the car. She refused. I held her arm and she attacked me, drawing blood. I knew Liz escalates if touched when she is angry, scared or frustrated. I knew my pushing her to do something would not help. I know my energy positive or negative will affect her ability to respond to complex situations."*

The Reality: 1. Liz is tactile defensive. Mom knows touching Liz when she is escalating only heightens the experience. Mom knew to back off and return after Liz cooled down. Police would not know that. 2. Liz is responsible for her behavior and not allowed to harm anyone. She will need to learn skills to manage feelings.

The Findings: Liz is guilty of the offense—she must learn not to be dangerous.

The Sentence: Liz is sentenced to house arrest with hard labor, glued to Mom for one month. The sentence can be shortened by one day for each day served with grace. No phone, no friends, no television. All social activities are only with family. Weekend work will be reduced to two hours each day.

Safe at home where life was secure, Liz got up each morning at 7:30 and worked from 8:00 am to 5:00 pm. She had two 15 minute breaks and one half-hour lunch. She learned many new homemaking and outdoor skills. Of course, this meant Warden Mom was jailed too, but we enjoyed each other and she was free in two weeks.

Braided together I was her mentor, coach and trail guide!

My family love just the way I am, but they make me grow, think and do hard things.

They are strict and want to keep me safe. Sometime I get mad about them being strict. MoM and I have secret Signals to keep me safe. One Signal tells mom I want her to say No. one signal tells me I am out of Control and if I want mom to tell me nicely I don't let her Signal two times.

if I don't pay attention to her signal she can yell at me.

We have special family signals that help keep our child safe.

One signal tells me no matter what she says she wants my no, to be no, and she is just saving face with her peers.

Another signal says "you are getting out of line, pull yourself together."

My children don't understand why they are being punished, let alone feel remorse. They feel sorry for themselves and think everyone is mean. Management is the key. The alternative is a downward spiral of punishment and misbehavior into chaos. We have discovered that corporal punishment perpetuates violence. Persons with FASD do not need exposure to violence as they model what they experience and know. We see the most improvement with loving instruction, continual management of behavior and then very gradual loosened control.

Diane, FASD mom

I feel like I am different.
Like I am not good enough.
Like others are better than me.
I want to be perfect but I can't.
FASD Life Expert teen

——

We talked openly. We wanted Liz to have as normal of life as possible.

Liz and I developed a secret "FAS alert" signal that signalled her behavior was crossing the line without letting others know.

PUSHING THE ENVELOPE

Prior to Liz joining our family, I was busy and active, always pushing the envelope. From entrepreneurial business success to two hundred mile Canadian wilderness white water canoe trips I enjoyed challenges. Now, for over ten years, I had Liz pushing my personal envelope—my patience, knowledge, intuition, human relation skills. She knew all my buttons and discovered some I didn't know existed. Often Liz's needs and behavior push my abilities against a brick wall leaving me with no energy to climb over, dig under or break down. Family and friends were concerned whether we'd survive parenting this dynamic child. Through these obstacles I came to rely on a personal spiritual relationship with God the Father and His Son Jesus. Many times I was left so empty that all I could do was pray to change me.

I worried if something happened to Karl or I, how would we, who would or could care enough for and about Liz. I initiated the first Designated Care Giver Law, (revised to the Standby Guardianship Law, 2002, MN Statutes, 257B.01-257B.10) and lobbied it through state legislature. This became the current Standby Guardianship (https://www. childwelfare.gov/systemwide/laws_policies/statutes/guardianship.cfm). Many States developed these laws specifically to address the needs of parents living with HIV/AIDS, other disabling conditions, or terminal illnesses who want to plan a legally secure future for their children. A standby guardianship differs from traditional guardianships in that the parent retains much of his or her authority over the child. is another alternative for transferring the custody and the care of children to another person.

Though I initiated the law, we had no volunteers to become Standby Guardians for our child. When we asked persons we thought were skilled to provide care, they laughed at us and shook their heads. Their plates were already too full.

I realized I was growing older and at some point Karl and I would face assisted living and independence choices for Liz. I decided to push the envelope back. I set the standard high and held her hand, knowing someday soon I needed to learn to let her go.

I immersed Liz in stimulation and experiences. I became her brain coach and life guide. Liz and I stumbled together discussing and processing ways to stand tall. We jumped into society and life with our swamp waders. We maneuvered through laundry, meals, housekeeping, buses and shopping. We tripped over time and appointments, finances and harmful friendships hoping to prepare for the future. I learned to check out an experience or environment before I gave a direction. I learned to teach tiny step by tiny step, stepping back when she didn't need me, stepping forward and catching when she fell. **Meanwhile the clock to adulthood kept tick-ticking.**

> My belief in Jesus is important to me. When I am alon or confused I can stop and pray and it helps me focus and think of other ideas. I like teen groups and I go to a teen church called the Rock.

The Ten Commandments

	SIMPLE MEANING	LEARN
1.	Trust God	Trust
2.	Worship only God	To think beyond myself
3.	Respect God's name	Power of God's name and words
4.	Rest and think about God	To take care of myself & keep myself healthy
5.	Respect and love your parents	Obedience
6.	Protect human life	To protect life
7.	Be true to your future husband or wife	The value of a promise
8.	Don't take what belongs to others	Honesty
9.	Don't lie about others	Truth
10.	Don't want what others have	To be satisfied

For Liz the 10 Commandments are not legalistic or oppressive. They provide her solid boundaries she needs to live safely.

I'm sure you get judgment everywhere else, you don't need it in the church. You made me stop and think—am I too quick to judge? We all need to be careful not to judge. Joyce

—

Liz and Sam have a deep faith based relationship. Faith provides a safety fence for success and a clear a set of rules to measure up to.

—

How do you find a church body that understands your child has hidden brain damage that causes unusual behaviors?

—

FAS SURVIVAL— *I see myself as a person who lives with FAS not just someone who survives it. However, one needs to remember that there are so many who are born with health problems as a result of FAS and there are many who don't survive. I use the term survivor because I know there are many who do not survive as a result of FAS.*

Charles Haire, FASD Life Expert
www.fassurvival.com

NO CONDEMNATION IN THE BODY OF CHRIST?

After we adopted Liz, we couldn't stay in the church we had been attending. At age two, Liz was very volatile, lost control at inopportune times causing commotion and judgment. Misunderstandings were pervasive. We didn't know what was wrong, so we couldn't help to make it better. Liz wanted to be part of Sunday School like other children. We had to move on.

Happily we found a church where children were mobile as long as they were quiet or participating in the singing, dancing or worship. This church accepted our family as we were and provided Liz the freedom she needed. During the teaching, the children colored pictures or did puzzles. During the worship, the children danced in the aisles, sang the worship songs, and waved colorful bits of cloth. Liz waved and jumped joyfully. I volunteered in the nursery, started toddler Sunday School, and listened to sermon tapes in the car. It was six months before I heard a sermon from the pulpit. Liz had fallen asleep.

One day, at age 13 Liz asked, "Mom, what is that hot feeling I get right between my lungs when it's something bad." The Holy Spirit had awakened her conscience.

I told her, "Honey, some people know right and wrong with their heads. You have a special connection with God that will tell you right and wrong inside of your heart. When you feel it, flee and ask God to keep you safe."

Liz brought her urban friends to our church by the carload. Even within our church's loving framework, they were easily singled out and unfortunately misunderstood and mishandled—their young spirits bruised and crushed. Embarrassed, defeated and hurt, Liz quit bringing her friends and attending church. She decided rollerblading was a better pastime and brought her carload of kids to the rink instead.

Thankfully, the church noticed and a teen outreach was started. One hundred and ten teens showed up the first evening. Liz's interest was piqued. "Who brought them," she wondered. She had to check it out. Rollerblades on, in she skated—making a visual 'skatement'—of will you accept me as I am? She was embraced back in love. The hearts of the congregation welcomed her, a member of the new generation. I think God laughed.

During her very unsafe adult transition, documented in her journals in *Braided Cord Tough Times In and Out* her faith and pray life increased. By the grace of God, she was kept alive and survived. As an adult, Liz uses the power of prayer to get through each day, find lost items, settle her emotions and pause long enough to enjoy reflective thought. Her faith life and that of her future husband is a high priority in their relationship and they are active and beloved in their church body.

> My room is my private space. I can let people in but it is mine. No boyz are allowed because mom said no I like to listen to Mya, Aaliyah, Mariah carey, cashmoney Records, No limit, Monica, Britney Spears, destinys child, and much more. I know many songs And like to sing I even sing In front of our whole church.

We discovered that the more our daughter is aware of her body, the less intrusive her body placement is to others. Understanding personal space and boundaries may be difficult for many neurologically injured persons to understand.

It may help to role play the following special places of common space invasion.

- *How to stand in a line*
- *Greeting people for the first time*
- *Saying goodbye to people you know well*
- *Saying goodbye to people you hardly know*
- *Interrupting a conversation*
- *Sitting on a public transportation*
- *Using public rest rooms*

We also discovered how important having her own private space is in order for her respect ours.

FASD is an organic brain disorder. It is not a psychiatric disorder. The central nervous system disorders, growth deficiencies and anti-social behaviors come as part of the package.

Perhaps we will discover new ways to make neural connections and provide her better problem-solving skills, an ability to encode information, and a way to enhance her visual and spatial skills.

> We did.
> Our FAScinating Journey

How do I keep Liz safe as a teen years so that she enters adulthood with the least secondary disabilities?

> We didn't.
> Braided Cord Tough Times In and Out

How do I teach her the gentle art of living and the dance of life?

> We're trying.
> Live Abilities at Better Endings.

Perhaps in time there will be a loving spouse or life coach to walk along side and guide her.

> Meet Sam.

Perhaps?

CHOICE AND CONSEQUENCE

Choices and consequences lie at the core of our parenting strategy. Liz was three when David moved on. The car with his new foster mother arrived to take him away. I buckled him into a car seat, hugged and kissed him good-bye and walked in the house.

Then as the tears flowed from my eyes, my little Elizabeth softly said, *"Don't cry mommy. He's gone. You know what the problem with babies is? They can't make choices. If he could make choices, he'd still be here."*

Liz has been raised with choices. She also has had to live with the aftermath of the consequences of her actions. If she is exposed to limited stress and allowed time to think, she can often make good decisions. The problems arise when she is faced with a new situation, is surrounded by peer pressure, or is stressed. That is not much different from most teens. What is different is her choices are 'off the deep end' beyond normal comprehension. She doesn't grasp the subtle difference between playing, story making and truth. When friends say everyone is doing it, with childlike naivete, she determines she should immediately partake in the noteworthy adventure. And peer encouragement and praise tended to override all parenting input.

If a friend is across the street and says come on over, she may run across the street without ever looking to see if a car is heading her way. When a light switch doesn't turn on immediately, the switch is destined for annihilation. This impulsivity without restraint is what gets persons with FASD mistakenly labeled behavior disordered instead of regulatory disordered. They get placed into groups that have behavior disordered persons in them with discipline techniques that don't work for neurologically impaired people.

Negative news, political and legislative issues, violent movies or games can place a tape recorder of voices and video of pictures in her head. As an adult, Liz shares that AA adds to her thinking of drinking instead of removes it.

People with FASD will shut down and stop trying to succeed if they are constantly met with failure and hostility. They may behave in ways that seem to provoke anger and hostility from others, or they may act out the very hostility they have experienced on innocent persons or animals. It is a vicious downward spiral—their desire to be kind and good masked with the pain of overriding and constant misunderstanding and defeat.

It is vital that we as a society begin to understand fetal alcohol exposure and train individuals who provide education, health care, justice, counseling, and personal care how to care about and for the individual with FASD. Together we need to discover strategies that work to help persons like Liz make choices to maintain and keep control. Impulsivity without restraint can become murder.

some of my friends say I act stupid and say really bad things about me.

It makes me feel mad.

Some friends care about me and when I act weird they just say "OK Liz you can bottle down" or just act weird with me and we laugh and have fun.

We like to go rollerblading at Skateland. I am a really good Skater. I like to go fast.

I also like to bikeride and hang out with my friends. We go to the park and swing on swings and talk.

We protect our daughter as much as we can with monitoring and careful supervision. We strive for open and honest communication. When she makes a bad choice, we help her deal with the aftermath. We worry about what will happen in adulthood. Will independence be possible or will it destroy her?

- **Read Braided Cord Tough Times In and Out by Liz Kulp**

2012 Finalist USA Best Books - Health Addictions and Recovery - Mom's Choice Gold Life Challenges)

I found all the jewelry she had stolen. I was sick. She has been stealing forever and she could have been arrested. I should be prepared for this type of behavior. No matter how much we know it is so hard to accept.

Sharon, FASD mom

———

Liz is a kick! She loves life and is giving it her all, the way she thinks life is. If others don't agree, she just continues on her agenda. She doesn't judge others. Things are just the way they are. Liz and a lot of other kids have this certain kind of innocence that all of us 'normal' folk could learn from.

Toni Hager, CanLearn Academy

———

God must be laughing as you are trying to raise Liz.
. . .I'll never forget the day she sucked her magnetic nose ring up her nose as we were driving and the resulting explosion. (R)
. . .I'll never forget going to the concert and having Liz hop over the back of the chair and run lost into the general public. (L)
. . . I'll never forget…giggle, giggle, oh my!(K)

Mom's Friends
are still laughing

PEERLESS FAUCETS

As Liz has grown older, friends she held dear have abandoned her. Perhaps fled is a better term. Her unexpected behavior and impulsive statements left them lying in ruins along life's road. Her unusual choices and dangerous actions left them shaking their heads. Neurological brain damage is difficult for parents to comprehend let alone youth. As fast as water can run through a faucet most real friendships went down the drain. My daughter is resilient. She is a fighter and with the pain of each loss she grows wiser. The experience becomes written upon her heart when it cannot be written in her brain. As her confidant, brain coach, cognitive translator and life guide I gently and sometimes forcefully direct her through stormy waters to safety.

Dave (15) and Liz (17)

We have embraced the teenage metamorphosis of wild hair, creative make-up, clothes, avant garde music and adventure. As with each generation, her choices of uniqueness are not her parents. We realize they are her expression to find herself, and the safest place to find herself is within the love and guidance of a family. Liz needed more time and experience than most adolescents to reach a healthy adulthood. She fell and failed many times before she reached a reasonable level of interdependence.

It is our job as her parents to love her unconditionally as she faces and meets her challenges—coaching, guiding and walking alongside. We lift her up as she struggles.

Liz is an extrovert. She loves life and gives it her all. People are attracted to her, and she easily attracts the wrong people. She doesn't have the discrimination to know the difference. Everyone is a 'friend,' until she is discarded or betrayed—her heart broken. Liz deserves what each of us deserves—success, self-confidence, a sense of belonging, self-satisfaction and to be loved. In most cases, this means her environment must be modified to help her function within a safe perimeter as she develops coping skills so she is not trapped by her own behavior.

When we initially wrote this book, I gazed down the road five, ten or twenty years, and decided where I hope Liz could be and what things are truly worth fighting for. We are now at almost year fifteen. I have learned I cannot decide what she will do in any given situation, but I can decide what I can do. Unified, my husband and I can decide to choose our battlegrounds in loving, direct and understandable ways for her. There have been many nights over these years we have held each other close as we forge through the mire of FASD.

I didn't think friends would steal from me so told them I had $900. I had saved every penny for five years. my friends snuck in my room and took it. they showed off with it. Mom called the moms and we got some back and the boyz dug a big garden for mom in really hot weather. Now I spend all my money. I don't keep any so no one can take it. my friends always beg me for me for money I have worked hard for. I don't want to but sometimes I give them some. they don't give to me money. I don't know why.

Individuals with FASD often don't understand what money means or represents to others. To them taking $100 is the same as taking a penny. They don't understand the difference between purchasing power and why the rightful owner would be upset if they take it. On the other hand, they are just as likely to give every dollar and possession they own away.

Difficulty with problem solving is one of the reasons persons with FASD lie and steal. They may be sincere in wanting to tell the truth, but not have the connections to relate to others accurately. Or in wanting to please create fantasy. Difficulty with communication and auditory processing further complicates this. In addition, the way the child experiences his or her world because of sensory processing my be far different from a parents.

———

Ownership is abstract—they see it, want it, take it—and with limited impulse control to stop themselves it is easily picked up—then hidden because they know they should not have it. If someone says they can 'use it' or 'have it', it may mean it's their's forever. They may not be able to figure out how to buy or work for it because of pre-planning.

Ann Yurcek, author, FASD mom

———

What do you mean stranger? "He told me his name. He's my friend. She friended me on the Internet!" My child can be so starved for friends she impulsively calls anyone just to be with someone.

ANYTHING GOES – IN MY POCKET

Individuals with FASD are often five or more years behind in social and emotional development, and model the behavior they see. As a teen, Liz's maturity level was often overestimated and people expected things of her she was not capable of. It has been crucial for us to provide explicit guidance and safe activities by surrounding Liz with positive role models. While Liz was growing up, we hosted ten foreign exchange students. These young people usually provide healthy role models for Liz and give Karl and I a balanced view of more mature adolescent behavior.

I could not always keep Liz safe and she was easily manipulated by peers. I felt like a mama grizzly bear as I monitored friends, activities and free time. Through tragedies and betrayals she gained wisdom we could not teach her due to results of her poor choice making. Yet from these mistakes, she has became a thoughtful counselor encouraging younger friends not to make bad choices and defending others who are wronged. There is a high cost these young people pay for innocence and naivete.

As a teen, Liz's real friends tended to be two or more years younger and looked up to her. We found age appropriate activities for the younger friends that also fit better for our daughter. Liz is not the only child affected by fetal alcohol in our urban neighborhood, she was however the only one diagnosed. We embraced the culture of the neighborhood and befriended the young people. I set my standards high demanding politeness, common courtesy and standard American English. I held each child accountable for his or her behavior. It was not an easy task. I inspected what I expected and they knew it.

More than once I was knighted meanest neighborhood mom. As an adult, Liz shared, *"Mom, you're a middle mother."* I asked what she meant by that and she explained, *"You were always fun, but never let us get away with bad things. Remember when you made us go get paint from the park police and paint ALL the picnic tables in two parks and two cities because we wrote our names on two different tables. We had to paint all ten!"* We found solutions outside the box. Down the center of our dining room table I placed a baby cactus gardens to eliminate careless stretches across. Liz's phone had a timer. Three offenses a child was banned from our yard. We treated the children with respect and trusted with verification. We expected reciprocation for favors. Liz founded the inspirational group the Mo'Angels and for four years I was a roady with a minivan of teens.

Often anything not nailed down and some things that weren't have been discovered to have jumped in pockets. We locked up and hid what we didn't want stolen. I often offered up a simple prayer – *"Lord, whatever is lost, stolen, burned or destroyed, let it be found. Amen."* Remarkably finders appeared with the missing objects and a smile.

I usually hate going on vacations. I don't like leaving my home. I feel safe here.

My family went to Europe and I saw alot of things but it was very hard to be away. Mom and dad bought me a pillow and blanket so I could wrap up and snuggle in the car or air plane.

Mostly we go on motor home trips where I have my own bed.

Mom says we travel so I can learn and understand things better. She says I am a concrete thinker.

We manage the new environment while traveling as best we can.

- **We find quiet places to unwind**
- **We pack nutritious snacks and foods she can eat**
- **We pack books, tapes, games and music she likes**
- **We pack a surprise bag of fun things**
- **We stop for bathroom breaks often**

They told me I shouldn't be friends with Liz because she has dumb problems. I told them I have dumb problems too, and we dumb problem people are going to stick together.

————

Our kids have an amazing ability to bounce back from failure, disappointment and rejection. Sometimes I think their inability to read social cues, inferences, body language, and other non-verbal communications is a gift that saves their souls and insulates them from a society that isn't always very tolerant or compassionate.

FASD Mom on FASlink

————

We don't isolate Liz from society. We let the world experience our wonderful and complex daughter and we let her experience the world. When people 'really' get to know and understand Liz, they begin to realize normal parenting strategies simply won't work for her. Their initial flippant judgment of our inept parenting is washed away with sincere respect.

GETTING AWAY FROM IT ALL

Once you step onto the FASlane there is no exit ramp and traveling with a young person with a brain disorder does not set the stage for relaxation. It does, however, expose everyone to life beyond the edges of the home turf. Karl and I love adventure. We love the outdoors and the challenges of the sky and the sea. We love the regality of creation so Liz grew up hiking up and down trails sounding like an Indy 500 race car among the peace and serenity of the wilderness.

Homeschooling Liz gave us the freedom to pick up and go when we study a topic to provide hands-on experiences and adventures and we adapted our love of nature and learning to her needs of comfort and security by purchasing an old motorhome. The camper provided us the safety and comforts of home, with the flexibility and independence to explore. Whenever Liz was overstimulated, we returned to our home on wheels. By traveling in the motorhome, we were able to visit battlefields, explore beaches, caverns and waterfalls. We enriched our lives with history in living museums, geography on the road and nature in state and national parks.

Faced with a school district curriculum guide to teach Viking, Roman and European history, we decided to visit our previous foreign exchange students to create a backdrop for understanding. We stretched twelve-year-old Liz as we visited Iceland, Denmark, Sweden and Germany. We walked in Viking and Roman ruins, explored monasteries and castles, wandered through orchards and climbed mountains.

Although at each stop, we stayed with the families of sisters or brothers who had spent a year in our home, Liz was surrounded and struggled with lifestyle and language differences. Her behavior reverted to survival. Around her neck she hung her house key and a pacifier. Her main focus became "Is there food—when?" "Is there a bathroom—where? and "Where will I sleep? We worked hard to maintain her rest since transition and change are extremely difficult for her and our first purchase was a down comforter and pillow with sheets to match her bedroom at home. That made it clear from the first day she was returning home and she cocooned safely in that blanket. We always packed or carried food and water. The first stop out of the car was seeking the toilet.

Once Karl performed superhuman heroics as he swooped her off the departing train. Tired of waiting for the right train, her impulsivity and impatience led her to jump alone onto a Stockholm subway heading the wrong way. And she was standing right next to us! It was a miracle they got on and off before the door closed to whisk them away.

Hands-on experience proved to bridge Liz's understanding of her world and enabled me to teach her while we got away—but not off—the FASlane.

Everbody love camping trips but I hate it. it's cloed, it's uncomfortable the tents stink, the food makes me sick and everything is different than home. I do not like overnights for scouts or church

We went to the Bahamas. I like it because it was nice weather there were big beaches and the people were really nice to me. We had our own condo so I had my own space and mom could cook food I can eat.

Choosing to embrace the wonders of the world with a child who has hidden neurodevelopmental differences exposes a family to unwarranted public misunderstandings of inappropriate parenting or discipline techniques.

Our special high risk children do not need their lives further complicated by an unnecessary intervention or removal from our homes by child protection. It is prudent to develop a small parenting manual with approved and written strategies from professionals that you can share with other care givers.

Join our SOS Parenting Program for ideas you can use and share.

We discovered when we did neurodevelopment evals with Toni Hager that Liz had mixed dominance issues:

1. Visual processing difficulties affect the awareness of what is going on around her and the ability to interact socially.

2. Auditory inefficiencies make it difficult to follow directions, pay attention to what is said, and interact socially.

3. Behavior that is a reflection of auditory processing hinders her ability to make sense of her environment, take appropriate actions and achieve academically.

4. In addition, she is often disconnected from her feelings and unable to express reasons for outbursts or misbehavior.

And Toni said, "These could be remediated with the right therapies?"

Could that be true?

Liz is an experienced primitive camper and has survived numerous Boundary Waters Canoe treks, but church camp and Girl Scout camping were a whole different story. Liz often provides her own solutions to cope with environmental elements that present challenges. It didn't surprise me she claimed my car as her tent and chose not to climb to the mountain peak. In doing so, she kept herself and the other girls safe from her impulsive behaviors. There is usually logic in Liz's choices, though it may be a challenge to find or comprehend it until I step back to silence my unfiltered personal defenses or frustration.

We discovered a condo unit or our camper provided the same sense of security Liz had at home because by having a common home base she was able to generalize learned skills more quickly. We stayed in one place. We shopped for food. She ate without the overstimulation of a restaurant. She had her own bed. We maintained our family structure and schedule. In a condo community we alerted neighbors of our daughter's issues and they became friendly temporary braided supporters for a successful vacation.

Traveling with Liz is always an adventure. She has no internal clock. She lives in the now and time is abstract. Even as an adult she may not comprehend how it works. If we are to be somewhere at a certain time, she is just as likely to think she should begin getting ready as she is to be ready. On the last day of vacation her internal clock says "we are going home" and the day starts when she wakes up. Unfortunately, she is likely to wake to go to the bathroom at 1:26 am. It is the new day and time for 'everyone' to get up. So much for sleep. Fortunately, she lives in a family who manages well on process time versus clock time, for the flight home we will never be late.

Airplane travel is filled with intense sounds, smells and feelings. People are tightly packed together beginning in the long winding lines of Homeland Security and passing through with a child like Liz, "who asks a series of loud never should ask them questions" we are assured a proper wanding. Once in the air, a person with tactile defense issues may have difficulty with the limited space, turbulence and pressure changes.

As we are landing, Liz's ears filled with pressure. She was drinking spring water and took the bottle and poured the water into her ear. Then she shook her head and hit her head on the seat. At that point, the fumes of verbal four letter exhaust spewed from her mouth and she threw the bottle—still filled with water—into the air. It was now raining in the airplane. The seat next to me was drenched. As if nothing had happened, she shook her head and smiled, "Whew, that's better! I'm going to do that on every flight."

It is difficult to access each new situation and discover how it can become a 'teachable moment' for a safe and positive growing experience.

Sometimes I have to dry off first.

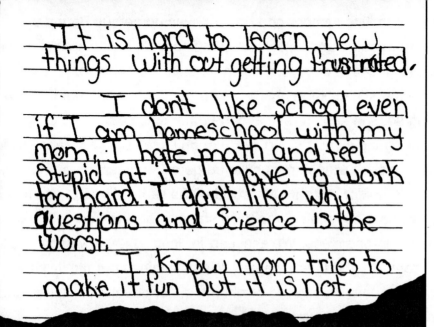

It is hard to learn new things with out getting frustrated. I don't like school even if I am homeschool with my mom, I hate math and feel stupid at it. I have to work too hard. I don't like why questions and Science is the worst. I know mom tries to make it fun but it is not.

The central nervous system has four main functions:

1. **To RECEIVE information through the three main sensory channels of tactile, visual and auditory.**

2. **To PROCESS (understand, interpret or categorize) this information through auditory and visual short-term memory.**

3. **To STORE into the long-term memory.**

4. **To UTILIZE the input.**

First the connections must be available !

Neurodevelopment philosophy implies a continuum of function ranging from a low of coma to a high of genius. All children are on this continuum.

It further believes that:

1. Function provides a mirror from which the level of development may be evaluated.

2. Development of the system follows an orderly sequence.

3. Everyone moves through the same development steps only at a different rate; some skip steps which can cause inefficiencies.

4. The most credible experts of any child are their parents.

Robert Doman, Jr.
www.nacd.org

We are indebted to the pioneering work of there astounding neuro-development and reorganization professionals in developing programs to help persons like our daughter to reach additional potential.

- Art Sandler   • Florence Scott
- Carl Delacato • Glenn Doman
- Bette LaMont • Toni Hager
- Judith Bluestone
- Lyelle Palmer
- Svetlana Musgatova
- Nina Jonio

PLATEAUS AND HORIZONTAL LEARNING

I structured Liz's schooling for success, but by age 13, it appeared we'd hit the vertical peak the psychiatrist warned me. Was there a way to press on? Or did I need to figure out horizontal learning strategies? I discovered Toni Hager on the Internet. She worked with the neural plasticity of the brain - rebuilding neural highways. She believed that "Academics are developmental levels. Toni had studied under Robert J. Doman Jr., director of National Association for Child Development (NACD). Currently NACD has over its thirty years of existence and work with over 30,000 clients, they do not specialize in FASD.

Toni wrote back, *"You are capable of teaching your child the academics of writing, reading and math, when the brain is at that level. If the brain hasn't reached a certain developmental level, it will not learn academics at that level."*

What level of development was Liz's brain? Could Toni tell me? I called her.

Toni was traveling through Minneapolis with a one hour layover at the terminal. I sent her Liz's manuscript for this book. She sent me all her articles. She laughingly told me when we met *"Liz is the first client I've had who gave me a detailed written history on her own. From what I already know about her, I have some things I can show you today. I brought you the 'Brain Builder' computer program and some training tapes so you can begin working with her immediately. I will be back through town in about a week. Why don't you bring Liz so we can meet."*

Neurodevelopment is based on the developmental profile. We look at the whole child and the profile represents functions associated with parts of the central nervous system. When the brain is given enough input, then it provides appropriate output.

"In order to help Liz, we needed to discover where the gaps in her development are." Toni did a functional neurological evaluation analyzing mastered skills and functions at each development level. She carefully noted which functions were absent or inefficiently performed to chart what part of the central nervous system was dysorganized. From this information she began to design Liz's program. *"Jodee, you need to know, there is no guarantee we can do anything, but I'm willing to try."*

On that first day, Toni taught me basic exercises to begin to build a neural highway back to Liz's brain. They were easy to do, didn't take a lot of time and Liz liked them. Liz and I began the new exercises and started working on Brain Builder, which we nicknamed Brain Buster. Her initial auditory and visual digit span began at 3-4. Liz had been processing her information at the level of a three to four-year-old.

If only this could help her!

Had our Creator made a blueprint we could build from?

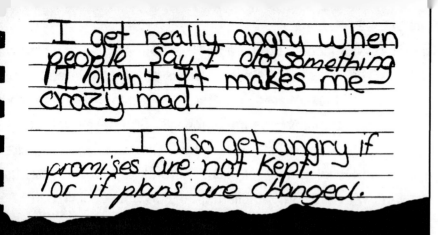

I get really angry when people say I do something I didn't. It makes me crazy mad.

I also get angry if promises are not kept, or if plans are changed.

In order for the brain to process information it must first have the ability to hold individual pieces of information together— short term memory.

- *The 'normal' two-year-old understands only two-step directions (get shoes, eat dinner, go ride) and speaks in couplets (want eat, no bed).*
- *A three-year-old processes three (simple phrases);*
- *A fouryear-old, four,*
- *And on up to a seven-year-old to adults. A seven-year-old or older should be able to understand seven bits of information. That's one reason phone numbers are seven digits.*

The individual above age seven who holds 3, 4 or 5 pieces of information together is struggling - to learn, to behave, to function in normal life.

Everything affects the brain to some degree. The brain's physical environment, general health, allergies, sensitivity, nutrition and respiration play an enormous role in the brain's ability to receive, process, store and use information. The real tragedy is that individuals are attempting to cope with unidentified neurological dysorganization that does not need to exist. Behavior is a reflection of auditory processing. Behavior is the ability to make sense from the environment, make decisions, take appropriate actions and achieve academically. A ten-year-old or adult who can process only 4 or 5 pieces of information will whine and throw a temper tantrum like a four or five-year-old when he or she is stressed, overwhelmed or being told, "No".

Toni Hager
www.canlearnacademy.org

In 2013, Toni Hager has worked with over 300 children who live with the challenges of FASD.

——

FROM LIZ — *"Mom, all that work we did made a difference. Thank you."*

Infants develop from head to toe, shoulders to fingertips, hips to toes and internal to external. Neurodevelopment looks at how the brain receives, processes, stores and utilizes information. Output is a reflection of input. The evaluation included the receptive areas of visual, auditory, and tactile channels including processing; as well as the expressive areas of manual (arms, hands, and fingers), mobility (legs and feet) and language. The evaluation also included social/behavior competence and nutrition.

Academics were assessed one-on-one with national testing standards. Liz (age 13) thought the evals were fun. **What we discovered was eye-popping.**

- Liz, who was a failure-to-thrive infant, had never learned to roll over or cross crawl, but she walked. No wonder coordination was an issue.
- She could not hop, skip or do jumping jacks, but she ran and jumped on everything.

Toni gave us exercises explaining that these skills also affected other development and life skills. Within two weeks Liz could cross pattern crawl, hop on one foot with her eyes closed and easily roll over. Her reading began to flow and **Liz requested opportunities to read.**

A Neurodevelopmentalist will assess these developmental issues:

Academic/Emotional:	Where on the developmental scale is the child?
Auditory Perception:	Does the child make sense of what she hears?
Spatial Awareness:	Can the child make sense of what is outside herself? Is she aware of her body?
Body Integration:	Can the child move in many directions? Can she wave her hands from one side of the body to the other (**midline crossing—horizontal & vertical**)?
Language:	What it the listening level (**receptive language**)? How can the child communicate (**expressive language**)? What is the quality of the child's sounds (**articulation**)? Does the child have an inner voice dialogue or is all communication still external?
Memory:	What level of short-term memory does the child have hearing (**auditory short term memory**) or seeing (visual short term memory)? What happens if you mix auditory and visual together?
Reflexive:	What reflexes does the child have? Are the early infant reflexes still engaged?
Time, Sequence, Organization:	(These skills are needed for classroom work.) What is the level of development of the child?
Visual Perception:	Can the child look and understand what she sees, rather than just being able to see?
Visualization:	Can the child make mental pictures?

HAGER NEURODEVELOPMENT VORTEX

EACH CHILD is very different and will require a different set of exercises, play and academics to help the child achieve new developmental levels.
Not all children can reach all levels, but improvements in abilities can be achieved thereby allowing the child an opportunity to become more self sufficient through learning, laughter and play.

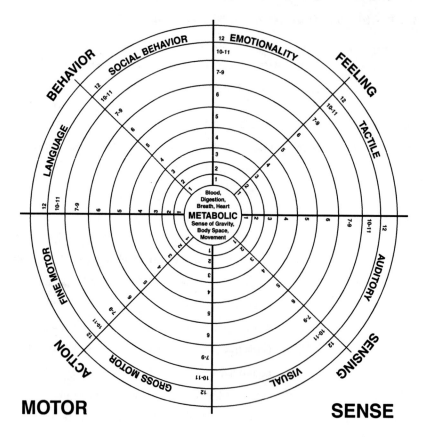

MOTOR   SENSE

11-12	Integration		5	Pre-Cortex
9-10	Frontal Cortex		4	Upper Midbrain
8	Cortex		3	Lower Midbrain
7	Cortex		2	Pons
6	Lower Cortex		1	Medula

MOTOR & BEHAVIOR OUTPUT comes from SENSE INPUT

For more information regarding the Hager

Neurodevelopment Vortex visit **www.canlearnacademy.org**

A child whose body is hypersensitive to touch will actually feel discomfort and stiffen or pull away from hugs. —Toni Hager

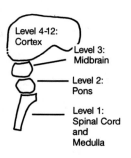

Level 4-12: Cortex
Level 3: Midbrain
Level 2: Pons
Level 1: Spinal Cord and Medulla

- Liz's pupils did not constrict or dilate when exposed to light.

Toni gave us exercises to help her pupils begin to open and close. At first, she had trouble opening her eyes for the exercises. Within a week she was less sun sensitive and able to use a computer without getting headaches. **She could begin to learn to type.**

- Liz lacked tactile sensitivity.

Toni taught us to utilize all the tactile senses - light touch, pressure, pain, friction, hot and cold. Within five weeks I was writing word messages on Liz's back with a feather. She was receptive to tickling. She had never had reflexes in her legs and they were jumping. **She asked me for a hug!**

- Liz had learned work-arounds in areas of basic academic skills.

Toni found the gaps I didn't know were there and taught us to fill them. Liz began developing automaticity in areas of word recognition and mathematics. **Reading became easier.**

- Liz was a mouth breather and her brain needed oxygen.

A child's brain needs 50% of the oxygen it takes in. She began to learn to breathe through her nose. At first she was afraid she die of suffocation. She lived, and walked, and soon sprinted while nose breathing. She was able to began to chew with her mouth closed. **Her father no longer had to wear the food Liz was eating.**

Liz Kulp at fifteen

This is Liz's brain map.

The darker grey area is where we begin in January 2000 and the lighter grey area is as of August 2001.

Thirty-one neurodevelopment exercises later, Toni said, *"Well, that's enough for this time. Let's see what Liz can do with these."*

At eight weeks into the program, Liz's digit span was a solid 5-6, a jump of two full development years. **We were not on a plateau. We were at the base of the mountain ready to climb with a new trail map.**

Note—*Liz worked with a number of skilled specialists in* Our FAScinating Journey Keys to Brain Potential Along the Path of Prenatal Brain Injury *(3rd Edition 2013) The Kulp family is grateful for their care.*

I am really good with hair. The people at the hair store call me Sparkles and like my ideas. I like to buy hair pieces and weave.

When I want to work with hair or be a singer or be an actress, or clothes designer.

I know it will take a lot of work to do that. I probably can not be everthing but I can be the best I can be.

Many find a solution to life's problems in a drink of alcohol. As you can see the result is far from easy.

We need to face the fact that alcohol does damage a child's brain.

Liz is a gift not just to our family but to the world.

- She has enriched my husband's and my life.

- She has stretched our minds, our personalities and our hearts.

- She has challenged us to be better than we ever had to be.

A Place in My Mind

Once upon a time
The sky was so bright
    in a place in my mind.
Days have passed
    and sorrow has come.
I'd like to take
    that time today, but
    time has passed away.
Dreams have died
    like someday you and I.
In my mind is like a dream
    just showing you how
    much you mean to me.
I know your face will
    never show a smug or
    tear deep inside
    how much you fear.
Your smile is like
    a rainbow
    with many colors.
I just want you
    to know
I love you so.

Liz Kulp
1/24/2000 her first poem

"Mom! I got a seven on Brain Builder!"

3/2/2000
seven weeks on program
    Our FAScinating Journey
    from 20 minutes to copy
    14 lines on a note card to
    a new Place in her Mind!

MOUNTAINS TO CLIMB

Our family has grown together on this FAScinating journey. Karl and I have learned to live, feel and understand Liz's world. We have set attainable standards and modified our environment to meet challenges head on with success. We are not always successful. The trials and struggles of parenting a child with FASD can be overwhelming. I am grateful to have a life partner to walk this path with me because I don't have the strength to do it alone. I give each day to my Heavenly Father, it's successes and it's problems. I Glorify God in the dark time and I ask for His wisdom, protection and peace. I am eternally grateful for His guidance.

Liz has been surrounded by support services and unconditional love. Ten years ago, we hoped a life coach or a spouse would eventually take the baton we hand over. Sam has embraced that role. Finally, neuro-research is gaining funding and discoveries are being made daily. The Internet has connected families, researchers, medical professionals, scientists, nutritionists, alternative health practitioners, neurodevelopmentalists, therapists and educators. Trailblazers have gone before us—doctors, scientists, researchers, teachers, judges, advocates, writers, therapists. We, with our children, have been the pioneers—planting and harvesting new ground in the fields of prenatal alcohol exposure. We have crossed the prairies. The mountains remain to be climbed and moved—we are now witnessing that movement from our Adult Experts living with the challenges of FASD. Their voices ring out the realities and unmask the misunderstandings.

Unbelievably in 2013, we are still arguing as a society about the reality of FASD and if a woman should drink while pregnant. Just ask Lz, her answer is, "Absolutely, NO!"

New Year's 2000, Liz asked me, *"Mom, what is your goal for the next ten years?"*

"My goal for the next ten years is that 65% of young people with FASD have successful lives instead of 10% like today." I answered.

"Mom, my goal is 90%. Sometimes I get mixed up and confused. I always try to be a kind and good person. When I get married, I want my husband to know everything about me and FASD so he can be supportive and understanding and not get frustrated by my behavior. Like when I act weird or lose control. Or when I feel horrible because I blow it or can't understand. I guess my boss will need to know about it, too. Because I get confused or frustrated. FASD is not going to stop me from living the best that I can. I love you, Mom."

"I love you too, Liz. You will be your best, I know you will." — Mom

BOOK 2
OUR FAScINATING JOURNEY
KEYS TO BRAIN POTENTIAL
ALONG THE PATH OF PRENATAL
BRAIN INJURY
BY JODEE KULP

Our FAScinating Journey is the continued story of our families journey into homeschool and neuro development. Revised in 2012, we have added current reference materials and up to date research. Follow Liz as she gain skills and exposes her community to the realities of living with the challenges of Fetal Alcohol Spectrum Disorders.

2012 Gold Mom's Choice - Special Needs Parenting

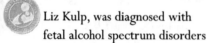

BOOK 3
BRAIDED CORD
TOUGH TIMES IN AND OUT
BY LIZ KULP

Liz Kulp, was diagnosed with fetal alcohol spectrum disorders (FASD) as a young teen. Knowing her challenges and understanding her strengths helped her graduate from public high school and strive to move on to independent adulthood like her peers. But, she soon learned that life within the context of a family that understood and helped her gain the desire for independence had not prepared her to live in a world filled with predators and abstract thinking.

Liz, unashamedly lets readers inside the hidden world of adult transition for many of our young people experiencing life with FASD. It is through her struggles the reader comes to understand the need for community awareness and the braiding of lives together. It is a story you will not soon forget. Liz Kulp was awarded the Canadian Starfish Award for her courage to build FASD awareness.

2010 Gold Mom's Choice - Adult Books - Life Challenges
2011 Silver Award About.com Special Needs Children

ALL OUR BOOKS ARE AVAILABLE AT
FASDBOOKSTORE.COM

I BELIEVE IN
LIVE ABILITIES
CHECK OUT OUR NEW PROGRAM

AND . . . It's gotta be FUN!

BRAIDED CORD
Excerpt from Liz.

"I was born an addict and ever since I was tiny I have overdone, overlooked or overwhelmed myself. I was born with fetal alcohol spectrum disorders, otherwise known as FASD. That means my mom drank while I was trying to grow in her stomach and because of her drinking some of my parts got mixed up and didn't grow too well. My differences are hidden and that's a real pain, because it is easy to judge a person by what you see.

The most difficult parts of my life are caused from my brain, which was probably the most affected. I have trouble learning new things and I live in a world that is louder, softer, harder, scratchier, noisier, shakier, slippery and more chaotic than most of the people reading this. I want you to imagine what it is like to feel the seams of your socks, the label on your clothes, the flicker of fluorescent lights, the mumblings and rumblings of every noise around you, and then try to learn new things.

Overwhelming.

Yes, that is what it is often for me."

Outstanding Young Leader **www.fosterclub.com.**
Liz's website is located at **www.braidedcord.net.**
For speaking, workshops or wholesale books contact:
www.betterendings.org

Liz Kulp is available to speak at your event to bring inside understanding into living with the challenged of FASD

Overlapping Behavioral Characteristics & Related Mental Health Diagnoses in Children

Overlapping Characteristics & Mental Health Diagnoses	FASD	ADD/ ADHD	Sensory Int. Dys.	Autism	Bi-Polar	RAD	Depres- sion	ODD	Trauma	Poverty
	Organic	Organic	Organic	Organic	Mood	Mood	Mood	Mood	Environ	Environ
Easily distracted by extraneous stimuli	X	X								
Developmental Dysmaturity	X			X						
Feel Different from other people	X				X					
Often does not follow through on instructions	X	X					X	X	X	X
Often interrupts/intrudes	X	X	X	X	X		X			X
Often engages in activities without considering possible consequences	X	X	X	X	X					X
Often has difficulty organizing tasks & activities	X	X		X	X		X			X
Difficulty with transitions	X		X	X	X					
No impulse controls, acts hyperactive	X	X	X		X	X				
Sleep Disturbance	X				X		X		X	
Indiscriminately affectionate with strangers	X		X		X	X				
Lack of eye contact	X		X	X		X	X			
Not cuddly	X			X		X	X			
Lying about the obvious	X				X	X				
No impulse controls, acts hyperactive	X		X		X	X			X	
Learning lags: "Won't learn, some can't learn"	X		X				X		X	X
Incessant chatter, **or** abnormal speech patterns	X		X	X	X	X				
Increased startle response	X		X						X	
Emotionally volatile, often exhibit wide mood swings	X	X	X	X	X	X	X	X	X	
Depression develops, often in teen years	X	X				X			X	
Problems with social interactions	X			X	X		X			
Defect in speech and language, delays	X			X						
Over/under-responsive to stimuli	X	X	X	X						
Perseveration, inflexibility	X			X	X					
Escalation in response to stress	X		X	X	X		X		X	
Poor problem solving	X			X	X		X			
Difficulty seeing cause & effect	X			X						
Exceptional abilities in one area	X			X						
Guess at what "normal" is	X			X						
Lie when it would be easy to tell the truth	X				X	X				
Difficulty initiating, following through	X	X			X		X			
Difficulty with relationships	X		X	X	X	X	X			
Manage time poorly/lack of comprehension of time	X	X			X		X			X
Information processing difficulties speech/language: receptive vs. expressive	X			X						
Often loses temper	X		X		X		X	X	X	
Often argues with adults	X				X			X		
Often actively defies or refuses to comply	X				X			X		
Often blames others for his or her mistakes	X	X			X		X	X		
Is often touchy or easily annoyed by others	X				X		X	X		
Is often angry and resentful	X						X	X		

Cathy Bruer-Thompson, Adoption Training Coordinator, Hennepin County, MN   612-543-0014   cathy.bruer-thompson@co.hennepin.mn.us   1/08
With much appreciation to the many who edited and contributed

References and Resources for "Overlapping Behavioral Characteristics and Related Mental Health Diagnoses in Children"

Diane Malbin: Clinical social worker, program developer, nationally recognized trainer on FASD and consultant, co-founder of FASCETS (Fetal Alcohol Syndrome Consultation)
   www.facets.org

MOFAS (Minnesota Organization on Fetal Alcohol Syndrome): **www.mofas.org**

NAMI: National Alliance on Mental Illness - fact sheets on mental health diagnoses, characteristics, medications, resources, local support groups for many mental illnesses
   www.nami.org/Template.cfm?Section=By_Illness
- Attention Deficit Hyperactivity Disorder
- Autism Spectrum Disorder
- Bi-Polar Disorder
- Reactive Attachment Disorder
- Obsessive-Compulsive Disorder
- Post Traumatic Stress Disorder

Bruce D. Perry, M.D., Ph.D.: Senior Fellow of The ChildTrauma Academy
   His neuroscience research has examined the effects of prenatal drug exposure on brain development, the neurobiology of human neuropsychiatric disorders, the neurophysiology of traumatic life events and basic mechanisms related to the development of neurotransmitter receptors in the brain.

Bessel van der Kolk, MD: clinician, researcher and teacher in the area of post traumatic stress and related phenomena, Medical Director of The Trauma Center, a program of Justice Resource Institute
   "Developmental Trauma Disorder: A New Rational Diagnosis for Children With Complex Trauma Histories," by Bessel van der Kolk, *Psychiatric Annals,* May 2005.

   "Complex Trauma in Children and Adolescents," Cook, Spinazzola, Ford, Lanktree, Blaustein, Cloitre, DeRosa, Hubbard, Kagan, Mallah, Olafson, van der Kolk, 2005, Psychiatric Annals, pp. 390-398- *Psychiatric Annals,* May 2005.

   Also *"Attachment, Self-regulation and Competency (ARC)"*

Mayo Clinic: Reactive Attachment Disorder Symptoms
   **www.mayoclinic.com/health/reactive-attachment-disorder/
   DS00988/DSECTION= symptoms**

Walter D. Buenning, PhD, Licensed Psychologist
Reactive Attachment Disorder Child Checklist of Characteristics
   www.reactiveattachmentdisordertreatment.com/childattachchecklist.pdf

Ruby K. Payne, Ph.D.: *A Framework for Understanding Poverty and Bridges Out of Poverty*
   Research focuses on the effects of poverty on students, families, and communities and how to better understand and support people from all economic backgrounds

In addition this document was reviewed for accuracy by several Minnesota experts in Children's Mental Health and Fetal Alcohol Spectrum Disorders

FASD RESOURCES FOR FAMILIES

ARTICLES, BOOKS & FILMS

FASD
knowledge is power

FASD—children ages 3+

 Winokur, Donnie Kanter *NUZZLE Love Between and Boy and His Service Dog* (2011). Audio Version (2012) Better Endings New Beginnings

FASD—children ages 8+

 Winokur, Morasha *My Invisible World Life with My Brother, His Disability and His Service Dog* (2009). Better Endings New Beginnings

FASD—Youth to adult

 Kulp, Liz, Kulp, Jodee, *The Best I Can Be, Living with Fetal Alcohol Syndrome or Effects*. (2000-Revised 2012). Better Endings New Beginnings

FASD—Teen to adult

 Crossen, Jan, *9 Lives Trilogy—9 Lives, I will Survive, 9 Lives, Cat Tales, 9 Lives, Full Circle*. (2008) Dragon Publishing

 Kulp, Liz, *The Braided Cord Tough Times In and Outs.*(2010). Better Endings New Beginnings

 Kulp, Jodee, *The Whitest Wall (Novel)*(2008). Revised to meet High School Curriculum Standards (2011)Better Endings New Beginnings

FASD—Adults

Burd, Larry, Ph.D. *Children with Fetal Alcohol Syndrome. A Handbook for Parents and Teachers.* (1999) To order: Larry Burd, PhD, 1300 S. Columbia Road, Grand Forks, ND 58202.

Buxton, Bonnie, *Damaged Angels: a Mother Discovers the Terrible Cost of Alcohol in Pregnancy* (2004)

Crowe, Jody Allen, The *Fatal Link: The Connection Between School Shooters and the Brain Damage from Prenatal Exposure to Alcohol* (2008) Outskirts Press

Davis, Diane: *Reaching Out to Children with Fas/Fae: A Handbook for Teachers, Counselors, and Parents Who Live and Works with Children Affected by Fetal Alcohol Syndrome.* (1994) Center for Applied Research.

Dorris, Michael: *Broken Cord: A Family's Ongoing Struggle with Fetal Alcohol Syndrome.* (1989) Harper & Row.

Federici, Ronald M.D., et al. *Help for the Hopeless Child: A Guide for Families.* (1998) Federici & Associates.

Kleinfield, Judith & Wescott, Siobhan: *Fantastic Antone Succeeds! Experiences in Educating Children with Fetal Alcohol Syndrome.* (1993) Fantastic Antone Grows Up! (2000) U Alaska

 Kulp, Jodee, *Our FAScinating Journey; Keys to Brain Potential* (2013). Better Endings New Beginnings

Lawryk, Liz, *Adopting a Child with Fetal Alcohol Spectrum Disorder* (2011) OBD Triage Institute, Canada

Lawryk, Liz, *Finding Perspective, Raising Successful Children Affected by Fetal Alcohol Spectrum Disorder* (2005) OBD Triage Institute, Canada

Malbin, Diane: *Fetal Alcohol Syndrome.* (1993) Hazelden.

McAndrew, Carol, *Speaking And Learning the Fasd Way* (2006) Red Lead Press

McCreight, Brenda: *Recognizing and Managing Children with Fetal Alcohol Syndrome/Fetal Alcohol Effects: A Guidebook.* (1998) Child Welfare League

 Neafcy, Stephen, *The Long Way to Simple, 50 years of Living, Loving and Laughing as a person with FASD.* (2008) Better Endings New Beginnings

Norgard, Katherin, Hard to Place: A Crime of Alcohol (2006) Recovery Resource Press

Streissguth, Ann, et al., *The Challenge of Fetal Alcohol Syndrome: Overcoming Secondary Disabilities.* (1997) University of Washington Press.

Streissguth, Ann: *Fetal Alcohol Syndrome: A Guide for Families and Communities.* (1997) Paul H. Brookes Publishing Co.

Taylor, Jennifer Poss. *Forfeiting All Sanity: A Mother's Story of Raising a Child with Fetal Alcohol Syndrome* (2010) Tate Publishing

 Yurcek, Ann *Tiny Titan, Journey of Hope*, (2007) Better Endings New Beginnings

MORE CHILDREN'S BOOKS

Bobula, Jill and Bobula, Katherine, *Forgetful Frankie, The World's Greatest Rock Skipper, Fetal Alcohol Spectrum Disorder,* (2006) Wildberry Productions Inc.

ARTICLES
research you can trust

Connor, Paul D. and Streissguth, Ann P, PhD, *Effects of Prenatal Exposure to Alcohol Across the Life Span* (1996) Published in Alcohol Health and Research World, Vol. 20, No. 3.

Kaimal, Shanti B.D.S., M.D.S., et al, *Understanding and Managing Fetal Alcohol Syndrome* (Feb 2004) Northwest Dentistry, Journal of MN Dental Assn.

Streissguth, Ann P, PhD, Barr, Helen M, MA, Kogan, Julia EdM, Bookstein, Fred L, PhD. *Understanding the Occurrence of Secondary Disabilities in Clients with Fetal Alcohol Syndrome (FAS) and Fetal Alcohol Effects (FAE)* (1996) Published by University of Washington School of Medicine, Department of Psychiatry and Behavioral Sciences, Fetal Alcohol and Drug Unit

Streissguth, Ann P, PhD, Barr, John S, PhD, Barr, Sampson, Paul D, PhD, Bookstein, Fred L, PhD. *Prenatal Alcohol Exposure and Family History of Alcoholism in the Eriology of Adolescent Alcohol Problems* (1998) Published at the Center of Alcohol Studies, Rutgers University.

Siever, David C.E.T., *The Rediscovery of Audio-Visual Entrainment Technology.* Comptronic Devices Ltd, 9008 51st Ave., Edmonton, Alberta, Canada T6E 5X4.   www.comptronic.com

BOOKS
you can understand

For Medical Professionals

Alters, Sandra, *Fetal Alcohol Disorders (Compact Research Series)* (2011) Referencepoint Press

Brick, John, Ph.D. *Handbook of the Medical Consequences of Alcohol and Drug Abuse* (2008) The Haworth Press

O'Malley, Kieran D., MD *ADHD And Fetal Alcohol Spectrum Disorders (FASD)* (2012) Nova Science Publishers

Soby, Jeanette, *Prenatal Exposure to Drugs/Alcohol: Characteristics And Educational Implications of Fetal Alcohol Syndrome And Cocaine/polydrug Effects* (2006) Charles C Thomas Pub Ltd; 2 ed.

ADOPTION/ATTACHMENT
get a better understanding

Keck, Gregory C. and Kupecky, Regina M, *Adopting the Hurt Child, Hope for Families with Special Needs Kids* (1998) Pinon

Magid, Ken Dr. and McKelvey, Carole A. *High Risk, Children Without a Conscience.* (1998) Bantum, Doubleday Dell Pub.

Monahon, Cynthia. *Children and Trauma: A Guide for Parents and Professionals in Helping Children Heal,* (1997) Jossey-Bass.

ALLEGATIONS
prevention and survival

Kulp, Jodee, *Families at Risk, a Guide to Understanding and Protecting Children and Care Providers Involved in Out-of-Home or Adoptive Care,* (1994) Better Endings, New Beginnings, Minnesota.

ALLERGIES & NUTRITION
we are what we eat

Block, Mary Ann, Dr., No More ADHD, *10 Steps to Help Your Child's Attention and Behavior Without Drugs* (2001) Kennsington.

Larson, Joan Mathews, PhD., *Seven Weeks to Sobriety, The Proven Program to Fight Alcoholism Through Nutrition* (1997) Ballantine Wellspring

Lyon, Michael R. *Healing the Hyper Active Brain Through the New Science of Functional Medicine* (2000) Focused Publishing.

Rapp, Doris J. MD, FAAA, FAAP, Bamberg Dorothy, RN, EdD, *The Impossible Child In School At Home?* (1986) Life Sciences Press.

Schmidt, Michael A., *Smart Fats, How Dietary Fats and Oils Affect Mental, Physical and Emotional Intelligence* (1997) North Atlantic Books.

BRAIN
books you can understand

Amen, Daniel G. M.D., *Change Your Brain, Change Your Life, The Breakthrough Program for Conquering Anxiety, Depression, Obsession, Anger and Impulsiveness.* (1998) Three Rivers Press, New York, NY

Diamond, Marian, PhD., *Magic Trees of the Mind: How to Nurture Your Child's Intelligence, Creativity and Health Emotions from Birth Through Adolescence* (1999) Plume

Doman, Glenn J., *What to Do About Your Brain Injured Child?,* (1994) Paragon Press, Honesdale, PA

Elliot, Lise, Ph.D., *What's Going On in There? How the Bran and Mind Develop in the First Five Years of Life.* (1991) Bantam

Goldberg, Stephen MD, *Clinical Neuroanatomy Made Ridiculously Simple,* (2010) MedMaster, Inc., (4th Ed).

Levine, Peter A. *Trauma Through a Child's Eyes Awakening the Ordinary Miracle of Healing - Infancy Through Adolescence* (2007) North Atlantic Books

Levine, Peter A. In an Unspoken Voice How the Body Releases Trauma and Restores Goodness (2010) North Atlantic Books

Lyon, Michael R. MD, *Healing the Hyperactive Brain Through the Science of New Functional Medicine* (2000) Focused Publishing

Mate, Gabor, MD, *In the Realm of Hungry Ghosts Close Encounters with Addiction* (2010) North Atlantic Books

Mate, Gabor, MD, *When the Body Says No: Understanding the Stress Connection* (2010) North Atlantic Books

Mate, Gabor, MD, *Hold On To Your Kidss Why Parents Need to Matter More Than Peers* (2010) North Atlantic Books

O'Brien, Dominic, *Learn to Remember, Transform Your Memory Skills* (2001) Six time World Memory Champion, Duncan Baird Publishers, London

Robbins, Jim: *A Symphony in the Brain, The Evolution of the New Brain Wave Biofeedback* (2000) Atlantic Monthly Press.

Sacks, Oliver: *The man who mistook his wife for a hat and other clinical tales,* Summit Books, NY (1985) *An anthropologist on Mars; Seven paradoxical tales;* Alfred A. Knopf, NY (1995)

Stine, Jean Marie. *Double Your Brain Power.* (1997) Prentice Hall Press.

EDUCATION
ideas to help children learn

Blow, Susan E., Elliot, Henrietta R. *The Mottoes and Commentaries of Friedrich Froebel's Mother Play.* (1895) D. Appleton and Company. New York

Campbell, Don G. & Brewer, Chris. *Rhythms of Learning Creative Tools for Developing Lifelong Skills.* (1991). Zephyr Press

Greenspan, Stanley I M.D. & Wieder, Serena PhD: *The Child with Special Needs Encouraging Intellectual and Emotional Growth.* (1998) Perseus Books.

Greenspan, Stanley I M.D. with Breslau, Nancy Lewis: *Building Healthy Minds, The Six Experiences that Create Intelligence and Emotional Growth in Babies and Young Children* (1999) Perseus Books.

Kline, Peter. *The Everyday Genius, Restoring Children's Natural Joy of Learning—And Yours Too.* (1988) Great Ocean Publishers, 1823 North Lincoln Street, Arlington, VA 22207.

Mauro, Terri, *50 Ways to Support Your Child's Special Education: From IEPs to Assorted Therapies, an Empowering Guide to Taking Action, Every Day* (2009) Adams Media

Tobias, Cynthia Ulrich. *Every Child Can Succeed.* (1996) *The Way They Learn* (1994) Focus on the Family Publishing

Shapiro, Lawrence E., PhD: *How to Raise a Child with High EQ, A Parents Guide to Emotional Intelligence.* (1998) Harper Perennial.

Wright, Peter W.D. and Darr Wright, Pamela, *Wrightslaw: All About IEPs* (2010) Harbor House Law Press

FUN creative
discipline ideas

Arp, Dave and Claudia, *60 One-Minute Memory Makers, Fun and Easy Ways to Create Family Memories that Last a Lifetime.* (1993) Thomas Nelson Publishing, Nashville, TN

Jasinek, Doris and Bell-Ryan, Pamela, *How To Build a House of Hearts, A Heart Level Home Makes Everyone Who Lives There Feel Good.* (1988) Comp Care, MN

Keating, Kathleen, *The Hug Therapy Book,* (1983) Comp Care, MN

Lansky, Vicki, *101 Ways to Tell Your Child "I Love You",* (1988) Contemporary Books, Chicago, IL

Simons, Laurie M.A. *Taking "No" for an Answer and Other Skills Children Need. Fifty Games to Teach Family Skills.* (2000) Parenting Press Inc., PO Box 75267, Seattle, WA 98125

St. Claire, Brita, *99 Ways to Drive Your Child Sane* (1999) Great ideas for dealing with RAD children. Order: Brita St. Claire, Families By Design, PO Box 2812, Glenwood Springs, CO 81602

ORGANIZATION
to make your life easier

Aslett, Don, (1984) *Clutter's Last Stand, It's Time to Dejunk Your Life!* Writers Digest Books, Cincinnati, OH

Barnes, Emilie, (1995) *Emilies Creative Home Organizer,* Harvest House, Eugene, OR

Campbell, Jeff, (1991) *Speed Cleaning Clean Your Home in Half the Time or Less!* Dell Books, New York, NY

SENSORY INTEGRATION
normalizing the senses

Ayres, A. Jean, *Sensory Integration and Your Child.* (1979) Western Psychological Services

Heller, Sharon, *Too Loud, Too Bright, Too Fast, Too Tight* (2003) Quill

Mauro, Terri, *The Everything® Parent's Guide to Sensory Integration Disorder, Get the right diagnosis, understand treatments, and advocate for your child* (2006) Adams Media

Kranowitz, Carol Stock, M.A., *The Out of Sync Child Recognizing and Coping with Sensory Integration Dysfunction.* (1998) Skylight Press *The Out of Sync Child Has Fun* (2003) Perigee

Schneider, Catherin Chemin, *Sensory Secrets* (2001) Concerned Communications.

Quirk, Norma J. MS, OTR, and DiMatties, Marie E., MS, OTR (1990) *The Relationship of Learning Problems and Classroom Performance to Sensory Integration.* Order: Nancy Quirk, 131 Dumas Road, Cherry Hill, NJ 08003.

UNITED PARENTING
keeping it together

Best, Denise, L. L.M.H.C. *"Therapeutic Parenting Manual for Adopted Children"©* (2012) www.parentingadoptedkids.com

Coleman, Paul, Dr., *How to Say It to Your Kids: The Right Words to Solve Problems, Soothe Feelings and Teach Values.* (2000) Prentice Hall Press.

Eyre, Richard and Linda. *Teaching Your Children Values* (1993) Fireside. Richard and Linda Eyre have a series of Teaching Your Children and they are all wonderful.

MacLeod, Jean, and Macraw, Sheena Macrae *Adoption Parenting: Creating a Toolbox, Building Connections* (2006) EMK Publishing

Phagan-Hansel, Kim, *The Foster Parenting Toolbox,* (2011) EMK Publishing

Purvis, Karen B PhD, Cross, David R. PhD, & Lyons Sunshine, Wendy, *The Connected Child For Parents Who Have Welcomed Children From Other Countries, From Troubled Backgrounds, With Special Behavioral or Emotional Needs,* (2007) McGrawHill

Wyckoff, PhD & Unell, Barbara, *Discipline Without Shouting of Spaking, Practical Solutions to the Most Common Preschool Behavior Problems* (1984) Meadowbrook Press

Snow, Kathy, *Disability is Natural: Revolutionary Common Sense for Raising Successful Children with Disabilities*; Softcover, 640 pages, $26.95. Order: 1-866-948-2222

Family Viewing

- Feature Films for Families offers positive alternatives in film viewing. Help instill values for our children. Feature Films for Families, www.familytv.com

For older children consider watching:
- *The Miracle Worker* Ann Brancroft
- *Westside Story* (1961) Natalie Wood
- *Tim* (1979) Mel Gibson
- *Kids* (1995)
- *Forest Gump* (1996) Tom Hanks
- *Rainman* (1988) with Tom Cruise
- *Beautiful Mind* (2001) Ron Howard

Television shows for interpretation and values discussion with family
- *Dr. Quinn Medicine Woman*
- *Happy Days*
- *Little House on the Prairie*
- *Touched by an Angel*

SCHOOL CURRICULUMS

NO SAFE AMOUNT: Women, Alcohol and Fetal Alcohol Syndrome — Interweaving interviews with real teens who have experimented with alcohol, animated sequences demonstrating how a growing fetus is affected by alcohol use inside the womb, plus an up-close and personal look at a young woman, Liz Kulp, growing up afflicted with Fetal Alcohol Syndrome (FAS), this program clearly demonstrates the unique risks that alcohol poses to women. www.hrmvideo.com

UNDERSTANDING FETAL ALCOHOL SPECTRUM DISORDERS — Grades 7-college—Viewers meet Liz, a teenager who is afflicted with Fetal Alcohol Syndrome (FAS) because her mother drank alcohol during her pregnancy. FAS represents a spectrum of physical and emotional disorders that occur because of alcohol poisoning before birth. Liz tells her story, supported by powerful graphics revealing how the developing fetus is damaged by alcohol. www.hrmvideo.com

FAS: EVERYBODY'S BABY Teresa Kellerman. Educational Video about FASD 34:46 min. FAS Star Enterprises, Fetal Alcohol Syndrome Community Resource Center www.fasstar.com

JOURNEY THROUGH THE HEALING CIRCLE, Robin LaDue, Carolyn Hartness. Native American storytelling, a family resource.
1) *The Little Fox* (birth to 5 years)
2) *The Little Mask* (6-11)
3) *Sees No Danger* (12-17)
4) *Travels in Circles* (18-22)
Washington State Foster Parent Training Institute
800-662-9111.

FASD RESOURCES FOR FAMILIES

INTERNET SUPPORT AND INFORMATION

NATIONAL FAS DIRECTORY — www.nofas.org

International Fetal Alcohol Awareness Day
"Ring Those Bells" September 9 @ 9:09 am—www.fasworld.com

In the 2nd Ed. of Our FAScinating Journey the websites dedicated to FASD took up one single page. Thankfully, this is not longer the case. We have provided a selection.

NOFAS—National Organization on Fetal Alcohol Syndrome, www.nofas.org 34 Current Affiliates (4/2012)

International NOFAS Affiliates
Australia —
* NOFASARD www.nofasard.org
* Russell Family rffada.org
United Kingdom — NOFAS UK www.nofas-uk.org

United States NOFAS Affiliates
Alaska —
* FASALASKA www.fasalaska.com
* STONE SOUP www.stonesoupgroup.org
California—
* Beginnings www.beginningsofslo.org
* CALFAS & FASD Connection
Georgia —NOFAS Georgia www.nofasgeorgia.org
Kentucky—Bluegrass Prevention Center www.kyfasd.org
Michigan—McFares Collation www.mcfares.org
Minnesota—MOFAS www.mofas.org
Ohio—Double Arc www.doublearc.org
Oregon—FASCETS www.fascets.org
Tennessee —
* Papillion Center for FASD www.papillioncenter.org
Utah — www.utahfetalalcohol.org
Washington—www.nofaswa.org
Wisconsin —
* Orchids FASD Services www.orchidsfasdservices.org
* FEN—pregnancyandalcohol.org

CANADA
* ARBI–Alcohol Related Brain Injury FAS/FAE Resource Site—www.arbi.org
* Asante Center—www.asantecentre.org
* FASD Saskatchewan—www.skfasnetwork.ca

* FASD Connections — www.fasdconnections.ca
* FASD One—www.fasdontario.ca/cms/

PARENT RUN SITES
* About.com Parenting Special Needs (Terri Mauro) specialchildren.about.com
* Better Endings New Beginnings www.betterendings.org
* FAS Community Resource Center www.fasstar.com
* ToolBox Parent www.toolboxparent.com

US SITES
* CDC – National Center for Disease Control www.cdc.gov/ncbddd/fas/ NIAAA—National Institute on Alcohol Abuse and Alcoholism www.niaaa.nih.gov
* MD Online Clinic— www.online-clinic.com/Content/FAS/fetal_alcohol_syndrome.asp
* SAMSHA—US Dept. Health and Human Services fascenter.samhsa.gov/

WASHINGTON STATE (Diagnostics)
* Fetal Alcohol and Drug Unit, Washington State — www.depts.washington.edu/fadu
* Fetal Alcohol Syndrome Diagnostic and Prevention Network, Washington State www.depts.washington.edu/fasdpn
* FASFRI—Fetal Alcohol Syndrome www.fetalalcohol-syndrome.org

FASD VIRTUAL SUPPORT GROUPS

Yahoo Groups —
* FAS Resource
* FASAdopt
* Russian Adoption
* Nutrition_for_FASD
* FASD Think Tank (private)
* AdoptionParenting
* NeuroNetwork
* GFCF Kids (Gluten Free)

FASlink an internet list service to help families dealing with fetal alcohol. Filled with great downloads.— Bruce Richie — www.acbr.com/fas/

This list is provided to give you a connection to links, support, education and information on fetal alcohol. It is by no means conclusive, nor does the author endorse everything these sites represent. Please see footnotes in manuscript for additional websites.

ANIMAL BASED THERAPY
- www.eagala.org—Egala Assisted Horse Therapy
- www.americanhippotherapyassociation.org—Hippo Therapy with Horses
- psychdog.org—Psychiatric Service Dog Society
- 4pawsforability.org—FASD Service Dogs
- www.TheChancerChronicles.com—Family with FASD service Dog
- www.Knarlwoods.com—K9andHumanKind Projects

BRAIN
- www.brainconnection.com—Simple to understand information about the brain. College credited online courses are also available
- www.thebrainstore.com—Practical resources brain research. (Free games for Kindle)

MEDICAL
- www.aap.org—American Academy of Pediatrics
- www.megson.com—Dr. Mary Megson, MD, specializes in Autism working towards returning children to health.

NEURO DEVELOPMENT

ASSOCIATIONS
- www.ndta.org
- www.neuroreorg.com

PROGRAMS AND ORGANIZATIONS
- www.braingym.com—Paul Dennison, Ph.D. Targeted brain activities through movement.
- www.handle.org—Judith Bluestone holistic approach to neurodevelopment called Gentle Enhancements. Three sample activities on her site.
- www.iahp.org—Institutes for Achievement of Human Potential

- www.developmentalmovement.org—Developmental Movement Consultants
- www.a4everfamily.org—A Forever Family
- www.neuroreorg.com—Neuro Developmetal Healing
- masgutovamethod.com—MNRI Method
- www.inpp.org.uk—The Institute for Neuro-Physiological Psychology. Peter Blythe and Sally Goddard Blythe.
- www.canlearnacademy.com—Children's Academy for Neurodevelopment and Learning. Toni Hager, NDS.
- www.llsys.com—Development of language software to help children with language issues.
- www.movetolearn.com.au—Barbara Pheloung author of, *Help Your Class to Learn, Overcoming Learning Difficulties* and *Help Your Child to Learn*. Books may be ordered from author's site.
- www.nacd.org—The National Academy of Child Development.
- www.specialyoga.com—Sonia Sumer of yoga techniques to enhance the natural development of children with special needs.
- www.stanleygreenspan.com—Development of emotional and social intelligence. Development of imagination, abstract and logic.
- www.retrainthebrain.com—Using the hand to speak to the brain. Jeanette Farmer a handwriting remediation specialist.
- www.zerotothree.org—Healthy development of babies and young children. Zero to Three, 734 15th St. #1000, Washington, DC, 20005. (202) 638-1144.

NEUROFEEDBACK
- www.isnr.org—International Society of Neurofeedback and Research
- www.aapb.org—Association for Applied Psychophysiology and Biofeedback
- www.qeeg.com—Behavioral Medicine Associates, Dr. John Nash Website. Qualified links are available from this site.
- www.eegspectrum.com—General site discussing neurofeedback
- www.neurofeed.com—Neurofeedback information
- www.crossroadsinstitute.org—Neurodevelopment center
- www.mindalive.ca—Brainwave Entrainment by David Siever

NUTRITION

- www.americanheart.org—American Heart Association site is filled with heart and brain healthy ideas and recipes.
- www.allergy.mcg.edu—American College of Allergy, Asthma and Immunology
- www.autismndi.com—ANDI Autism Network for Dietary Intervention. Support for families on gluten free and casein free diets.
- www.foodallergy.org—Food Allegy and Anaphylaxis Network offers a wealth of information.
- www.foodnews.org—Environmental Working Group—pesticide and toxic chemical load in daily food.
- www.gfcfdiet.com—Gluten and casein-free diet information
- www.pureliving.com—Dr. Michael Lyon, a functional medicine physician and author of *Healing the Hyperactive Brain.*

PARENTING STRATEGIES

- www.difficultchild.com—The Nurtured Heart Approach by Howard Glasser author of *Transforming the Difficult Child*. Recommended by Dr. Patch Adams.
- www.disabilityisnatural.com—Kathie Snow provides professionals and parents with a wholistic and healthy viewpoint of raising a child with a disability.
- www.parent-magic.com—*1-2-3 Magic* and creative strategies to help you to love and work with your child.
- www.nancythomasparenting.com—Families by design parenting idea by Nancy Thomas

SCHOOLS & EDUCATION

- www.actg.org — A Chance To Grow
- www.bced.gov.bc.ca/specialed/fas—BC Canada, FASD Teacher Resource Guide
- www.canlearnacademy.com—Kids Can Learn Academy
- http://idea.ed.gov/download/finalregulations.pdf—US Fed Special Ed Regs (current 2006)
- http://www2.ed.gov/about/offices/list/osers/osep/index.html — US Federal Office of Special Educaiton

SENSES

- www.hhmi.org/senses — Seeing, Hearing and Smelling the World. Howard Hughes Medical Institute.
- www.tomatis.com — Ear training site with information to help you understand this pioneering approach.
- www.mindalive.ca — Audio-visual entrainment program used successfully at A Chance to Grow New Visions School.
- www.advancedbrain.com — Programs for building working memory, CD's, The Listening Program. Alex Doman
- www.garylamb.com — Gary Lamb's 60 Beats Per Minute music.
- www.new-vis.com —Marvelous Mouth Music allows a child to go back to prespeech with musical fun.
- www.feldenkrais.com — The Feldenkrais Method teaches how we can improve our capabilities to function in daily life.

TRAUMA

- www..childtrauma.org — Bruce D. Perry, MD, Ph.D
- www.childtraumaacademy.com — Free online courses to help understand how children cope with traumatic events.
- www.traumahealing.com — The work of Dr. Peter Levine
- www.somaticexperience.com — The work of Dr. Peter Levine

OTHER THERAPY STRATEGIES

- www.upledger.com—Cranial Sacral Therapy
- www.callirobics.com—Handwriting support
- www.perlhealth.com—Hyberbaric Oxygen Therapy
- www.authentic-breathing.com—Breath Work
- antoniarathbun.com—Art Therapy
- www.randifredricks.com—Wholistic Therapies
- www.musictherapy.org —Music Therapy
- www.adta.org —Dance Therapy
- www.lighttherapy.philips.com—Light Therapy
- drummingforwellness.com—Drum Therapy

NOTE: *Each child living with the challenges of FASD is different and each professional working with your child will be different interaction—*

When you have Trust + Safety the child gets the "I did its!"

FASD RESOURCES FOR FAMILIES

FAMILY TREASURE BOX

Golden Learning Key
Trust with Safety allows "I did it"

- Discover your child's personality, learning and processing preferences. Respect individuality. Things that irritate you now may lead to a future success for your child.
- Teach them slowly. Teach them patiently. Teach them again and again. Do not sacrifice the quality of your teaching to encourage quantity. (When teaching housekeeping skills consider professional methods.)
- Talk about strengths and figure out ways to maximize them.
- Provide exposure and experiences. Coach and mentor them through life's challenges.
- Focus on positives rather than negatives. The impossible may happen and children can surprise us.
- Strive to keep our young people safe. Prevent exposure and experiences to: alcohol, drugs, pornography, violence.
- Allow freedoms as responsibility, judgment, new skills and talents develop.
- Show we value each person's work and provide opportunity for learning.
- Redirect enthusiasm without criticizing or squelching. Break a grandiose ideas into beginning small pieces. .
- Help each other deal with failure and bounce back without being devastated.
- Provide support systems.
- Provide logical consequences.
  - Keep ourselves healthy so we can be our best.

Accept FASD is going to change life in ways we cannot control.

Tips to find a child's treasures to build a Braided Cord for living:

- Where does your child find his/her joy?
- What are the child's keen interests or talents?
- Who are people your child relates well to?
- Are these people available to participate in the child's life (daily, weekly, monthly, seasonally)
- Does your child know something no one else in the family does? Let the child teach others a skill (dog training, fishing, sport, art, music, etc.)
- Does an irritating behavior demonstrate creative problem solving?

The Common Good Qualities below have been compiled from ARC Northland in Duluth (2004). Their sources were from Clarren, Streissguth, Morse, Malbin

- tactile
- cuddly
- friendly/happy
- spontaneous
- loyal
- trusting
- loving
- gentle
- affectionate
- curious
- persistent
- willing
- involved
- love of nature
- loving of animals
- enjoy gardening
- enjoy constructing
- kind
- caring
- helpful
- concerned
- sensitive
- athletic
- moral and fair
- artistic
- musical
- highly verbal
- rich fantasy life
- hard workers
- atypical strengths
- nurturing
- compassionate
- sense of humor
- committed
- devoted as parents
- determined
- strong sense of self
- creative
- social
- follows through
- good with children
- wonderful story tellers
- good long term visual memory

My child hates herself, thinks she is stupid and ugly...what can I do?

My heart breaks for the self-esteem of these children. They try so hard to cloak themselves in a mask of normalcy and then dive into a social abyss with their dismal behaviors. They are misunderstood, misdiagnosed and struggle with normal daily life issues. Go on a treasure hunt for the person you love.—post the treasure you fins on the refrigerator, give to grandma and grandpa! You won't regret it.

2012 Treasures from the FASD Think Tank

- I love my daughter's ability to help me see the world from a different perspective, herability of pick up on nuances of how one is feeling, her play on words: "egg-xactly" "egg-traordinary" and exclaiming "That is MY joke!" (Kathy)

- My husband is loving, kind to us no matter what, has a great sense of humor, always tries to do better, can laugh at himself and tries to help with ALL the chores, not just the ones he likes (Peggy)

- I challenged myself to come up with twenty things I love about my son (and it was fairly easy to do): My son is over age 20! (Victoria)
  1. his smile and laughter
  2. his friendship
  3. his 'child whisperer' abilities
  4. his music and dancing
  5. his ability to forgive
  6. his ability to research the internet for 'deals', comparison shop and find the best deals before he makes a purchase
  7. his ability to instantaneously work almost any electronic device
  8. his wonderful compliance in taking supplements and NR exercises when mom asks/asked
  9. his creativity and unusual/unique way of looking at the world; and opening my eyes to this uniqueness
  10. his voracious appetite and his culinary expertise
  11. his bravery....it takes this to live in a world that is often unkind to him
  12. his eagerness to share....evident since he was very young
  13. his brilliance at learning . . .all the things he is interested in.
  14. his ability to sometimes know what he is not ready for (eg., not ready to drive)
  15. his ability to recite movie dialogue and passages from books, like a savant (both wonderful and scary)
  16. his realization that if he's carrying cash, he will spend it but if it's in the bank, he's careful and willing to save it
  17. his kindness
  18. his love of animals
  19. his love of jokes and plays on words
  . his artistic talents

- I love my daughter's view of the world, she provides me with a truth I would have never understood and people I would never have known. (Jodee)

Quick Notes:

Music uses both sides of the brain for learning. One side for creating the music and one side for expressing it.
- Music at 60 bps (beats per minute) is near our heart rates and tends to relax a person.
- Music can change the atmosphere.
- Play with different kinds of music and notice its affect on you and your children.

Middle School is a hard time for teens living with FASD.
- It can take 20-30 min. to assimilate change leaving very little time for class work.
- Your school may have a program available to eliminate the chaos and make transitions less frustrating. An in-school suspension room with natural lighting may be a blessing in disguise.

FASD RESOURCES FOR FAMILIES

TEACHING TIPS—GENERAL

TEACH TO THE CHILD'S INTERESTS

Discover a child's desires

Lighting preference
- low light
- window light
- no light

Temperature preference
- open window
- air conditioning
- warm heat

Seating placement

Work
- alone
- with friend

Visual	Auditory	Kinesthetic
Flashcards	Tapes	Dice and Cards
Pop-up books	Music	Clay
Slates	Oral reading	Games
Copy work	Educational videos	Computers
Board work	Computers	Construction
Diagrams	Direct teaching	Experiments
Workbooks	Songs	Manipulatives
Readers	Plays	Field trips
Magazines	Drama	Pop-up books
Letterwriting	Oral drills	Tactile flash cards
Storyboards	Interviews	Typing
Pantomime	Skip count	Writing in sand/air

Things families can do for fun to improve a child's vision:

- **Dot-to-dot:** Muscle control, eye-hand coordination, creating and completion of task.

- **Mazes:** Perceptual path work, eye-hand control, planning, sequencing, pencil control, visualizing a path, solving an unknown, completion of task.

- **Hidden pictures:** Seeing a form within a form—perceptual training.

- **Word search puzzles:** Organization, ocular skills, visual discrimination, letter recognition, spelling and vocabulary.

- **Pattern blocks:** Spatial reasoning, visualization, develops problem solving.

- **GeoBoards:** Visualization, hand skills, bilateral control, perceptual skills, memory.

- **Wicki sticks:** Add flexibility and creativity for dot to dots and mazes.

- **Other Toys:** String games, pick up sticks, slinky, etch-a- sketch, making balloon animals: ambidextrous (two-hand) play.

Characteristics of Child with FASD

Deb Evensen (www.FASAlaska.com)

*Build
Safety*

*Create
Trust*

*Then you
get the*

*"I did it!"
and
"I can do it!"*

*Enjoy the
process
and
celebrate
the results*

*Change your
thinking to
brain injury
based
behavior and
learning
strategies*

*. . .
and don't
forget to
laugh and
dance and
play . . .*

Typical 5 year old	Developmental Age with FASD 5 years going on 2 years
• Go to school • Follow 3 instructions • Interactive, cooperative play • Share • Take turns	• Take naps • Follow one instruction • Help mommy • Parallel play • Active • My way or no way
Typical 10 year old	**10 years going on 6 years**
• Answers abstract questions • Gets along with other, • Solves problems • Learns inferentially, academic and social • Physical stamina • Generalizes information learned from • Worksheets	• Learn by doing experientially • Mirror and echo words, behaviors • Supervised play, structured play • Learn from modeled problem solving • Easily fatigued by mental work
Typical 13-year olds	**13-years going on 8-years**
• Are responsible • Organize themselves, plan ahead, follow through • Meet deadlines after being told once • Initiate, follow through • Appropriate social boundaries re: body space, appropriate touch • Establish and maintain friendships	• Need reminding • Need visual cues, modeling • Simple expectations • Need prompting • Kinesthetic, tactile, lots of touching, in your space, just learning about boundaries • Early friendships
Typical 18 year old	**18 years going on 10 years.**
• On the verge of independence • Maintain a job and graduate from school • Have a plan for life • Budget own money • Organize	• Needs structure and guidance • Limited choices of activities • In the "here and now", little projection Giggles, curiosity, frustration • Gets an allowance • Gets organized with the help of adults

**MN DHS
Guidelines of Care**
for Children with Special
Health Care Needs: Fetal
Alcohol Syndrome and
Fetal Alcohol Effect
recommends families
stress the following:

1. **Structure**—Create a
structured environ-
ment which includes
limited choices. Have
clear and set routines.
Adjust the environ-
ment for slower devel-
opment and under-
standing.

2. **Supervision**—
Carefully supervise
teens so they do not
place themselves in
dangerous situations.

3. **Simplicity**—State
instructions briefly
and clearly. Use sim-
ple directions and
orders.

4. **Steps**—Break tasks
down into small steps.
Teach each step
through repetition.
Lists may be helpful.
Use rewards as incen-
tives.

5. **Setting**—Teach
desired skills in the
way in which they will
be used. Teens with
FASD may not have
the ability to transfer
skills from one setting
to another.

MORE TEACHING TIPS

1. Keep yourself healthy.
Maintain the support of other teachers. Teaching children with FASD can
be very frustrating.

2. Be a team player.
The parents of a child with FASD will
have ideas of how to help you with
their child. Listen carefully to what
they have to say. Find a way to keep in
touch with the family on a regular
basis.

**3. Model and mentor correct
behavior.** Focus on behaviors you
want the student to grow, not on
behaviors you don't like.

4. Observe, refocus, reframe.
Misbehavior is often a neurological
misfire. Take a deep breath, think
about what might be going on. Is it
the child can't or is it the child won't?
Ask the child how you can help. You
may be surprised at her answer.

5. Give one direction at a time.
Multiple directions are confusing to a
child with FASD. The student may
forget what was said first, may not
understand what was said or may be
confused by a two or more part question.
a. Give clear directions—say "put
your coats on" instead of "get ready
to go."
b. Use fewer words—stop, walk, go.
c. Child can repeat back what you say.

6. Reteach, reteach, reteach Keep
it simple….if they are not getting it
break it down into even smaller pieces
or teach something easier to build
upon.
    a. Use repetition.
    b. Be consistent.
    c. Make smaller steps.
    d. Build on learning.
    e. Try backward chaining.

**7. Teach replacement
behavior.**
    —Reframe
    —Thought-stopping, positive
      thinking
    —Deep breathing and relaxation
    —Fun, humor and laughter!

8. Use Motivators. Encouragement,
positive attention, rewards and incen-
tives for appropriate behavior and
meeting learning challenges. Set a
goal to be accomplished. Some incen-
tives work well small toys, money,
time with friends, roller rink passes,
special dinners, and movies.

**9. Modify the environment
for the child's success.**
The environment is an absolute 'key'
to the child's success. Prevent the
meltdown from happening.
- Discipline yourself to be sensitive
to set up your child for success.
This may mean changing plans if
the child is too tired, irritable, or
nervous.
- Never go out hungry or over
stimulated.

TEACHING TIPS
DO I HAVE AN FASD CHILD IN CLASS?

adapted from http://www.lcsc.edu/education/fas/signals

External signs

1. Daydreaming for more than 50% of the class time
2. Bitten finger, finger nails and lips
3. Silence
4. Forgetfulness on an hourly, daily basis
5. Anger (quiet until puberty)

Internal signs

(what you may see)

1. **Confusion**
   a. What time is it?
   b. What class is this?
   c. What happened in this class the day, week, or mouth before?
   d. What is this?
   e. Where is my assignment? Is this finished?

2. **Emotional Breakdown**
   a. Tears, but no noise
   b. Retreat from everything, staring
   c. High anxiety, no verbalization*

3. **Sexual Activity**
   a. Marked increase as they become older
   b. Impulsive acts or inappropriate touching
   c. Will cause a sexual incident on a "dare"
   d. Consequences are not under stood, nor is a pregnant girl or girlfriend

Identified, Diagnosed with FASD

1. All the above will be the same
2. These students should have a letter from a diagnostic clinic or a note to talk to someone who knows their history

Unidentified Students with FASD

1. Seems lazy
2. Falls asleep in class on a daily basis
3. Continuously late for class
4. Poor eyesight
5. Small, skinny fingers, ears, or legs
6. Complains of pain in joints/headaches
7. Have history of normal physical problems in excess of usual occurrences (especially in head, kneecaps, fingers, ankles, and internal organs)

This changes as they become older, especially in boys.

- **Anxiety + Anger = Violence**, *sometimes to the point that it becomes a matter for officials or the police. While this can be disruptive and sometimes frightening for everyone.*

- **AVOID PHYSICAL TOUCH AS THE FIRST WAY OF REACHING THIS YOUNG PERSON.** *Talking quietly but in a steady tone of voice will be more effective.*

Braid into the life of o a Teen living with FASD:

1. Get to know your teen's friends and stay parent active
   — offer rides
   —offer counsel
   —offer activities
2. Find teen or young adult group and individual activities your teen can participate in and be accepted: scouts, choir, church group, band, Big Brother or Big Sister / rollerblading, biking, skateboards, Special Olympics, walking, running, swimming.
3. Involve teen in care of animals. Consider volunteering at an animal shelter.
4. Designate a mutually agreed upon friend or relative who will provide a safe house.
5. Designate a mutually agreed upon adult friend or relative who will be a mentor and provide an adult/teen activity once every six weeks or less.– hair appointment, concert, zoo, sporting event).
6. Delay obtaining a driver's license.
7. Find medical personnel who are willing to develop a relationship with you and your teen.

SEEING THE SMOKE SIGNALS BEFORE A RAGE

Jodee Kulp, published in Adoption Today

When was the last time you felt "real fear"? Was it when you spun out on a road and did NOT connect with another car or stable object? Was it when the elevator made a jump on the way up or down? Remember that feeling? How long did you remain in alert? Now that you can feel—helpless in doing anything about the possibility of impending doom—imagine what your child with atypical behavior and social experiences faces each day. Watch for your child becoming overwhelmed and notice subtle body changes. A rage response hijacks the mind and body and may even include a sense of relief or joy from the child in release of the pent up feelings. When a child is raging social perception, speech, judgment, and motor behavior is weakened. The child may not be able to remember the facts of the event. Following are some early smoke signals to help "before a rage" when you still have time to redirect, remove or change the environment in a situation.

Watch for the smoke signals
Do NOT fan the fire!

This is the time for calm or joyful redirection, refocus, patience, and healthy humor
- Muscle tension or sudden loss of muscle tone
- Heart rate increase
- Face or ears flushed
- Goosebumps
- Trembling
- Blanching of face,
- Breathing change
- Visual focus hard to sustain
- Deterioration of a task
- Crying
- Chewing on clothing

When to expect smoke signals
- School work they are unable to complete
- Conversations they are unable to understand
- Room temperature or lighting or scents they are unable to adjust
- Feelings are hurt
- Self-esteem shattered, insulted
- Unable to accomplish something
- Another person persists in annoying child
- Promise is broken
- Personal belonging removed or stolen
- Sensory overloaded area
- Pressed for time
- Too many steps in a process
- Seeing no progress in what they are doing

A child may shut down or ramp up

Shut down
- Very shallow breathing
- Rocking
- Nodding head in agreement
- Staring or glaze look
- Voice volume decrease
- Head lowered
- Saying "Thank You" for helping me

Ramp up
- Rapid breathing
- Shaking head in disagreement
- Pacing or humming sound
- Clenched fists
- Head up
- Voice volume increase

"God never promises to remove us from our struggles. He does promise, however, to change the way we look at them."
Max Lucado

"When I was a child learning to control rages I would get so tense I would shake. My father thought I was having seizures, but it was simply trying to gain control." Ken Moore - FASD Life Expert

FASD RESOURCES FOR FAMILIES FROM FAMILIES

Information for Families and Friends

By Jodee Kulp written to help people understand.

We need you! Children with brain injury need non-judgmental, loving friends and relatives who accept them as they are, encourage but not demand growth, and rejoice in strengths and accomplishments no matter how small.

What every child with FASD needs?
- Unconditional love.
- Acceptance.
- Attention.
- Supervision.
- Patience and understanding.
- Wisdom.
- Structure / environmental controls.
- Redirection.
- Help to slow down when getting out of control (deceleration).
- Someone who believes they are capable.

We need your help. It is exhausting to raise a child who has prenatal brain injury. Consider learning how to provide respite for us. Please understand this is a brain injury not an issue of 'bad' parenting and our child is not a 'bad' child.

Ways to help our child grow
1. Praise their strengths.
2. Acknowledge their expression of frustration.
3. Respect their fears and difficulty with change.
4. Understand that behaviors may be a can't do it not a won't do it.
5. Talk to them as a person - not someone who is stupid.
6. Keep from comparing them with others.
7. Keep from joking, teasing or putting them down.
8. Keep yourself from telling them, "you will grow out of this."
9. Get involved in their interests.
10. Find out what they are trying to learn and think of fun ways to join.

We may have to avoid
- Holidays and birthdays
- Circus, concerts, movies, sport events
- These events may be too much for our child to handle.
- New people or visitors in the home are a change in routine and may be difficult for the child.

Think different birthdays
Birthdays can be very overwhelming:
- Let the child pick out their own presents and don't wrap them. The energy of the surprise may be hard for child to handle.
- Start the day with a special breakfast and a few tiny presents.
- Wear matching family T-shirts on holidays, community events and birthdays.
- If you have a party keep it organized and simple.
- Have the child pick their favorite dinner.

Think different holidays and events
- New Years Party on the child's time zone while they're still awake. Make a time capsule using a can with a lid. Write a New Years wish. Put a picture of the child, favorite toy, food, color, story. Open the capsule next New Year to see how much they have changed.
- Adopt a family for a holiday, visit a shelter to deliver presents
- Have a holiday tea party with the family - tea, cookies or appetizers
- Make a paper chain the child can rip off a chain per day to count down to the holiday or write a number count down on a calendar and cross off days.
- Valentines Day everyone in family writes or says three nice thing about every other family member.
- Thanksgiving Trees from Nov. 1 to 31 secretly place paper leaves with notes of thanksgiving on a bare twig tree.

- Have a pajama day. Stay home, goof off and do things together.
- Develop a bedtime or wake up ritual.

Chores

1. Teach the child the best way you know how to do the chore. First learning is very important to children with FASD. Realize child may not be able to cross midline so sometimes ability may be not yet possible.
   - Use very small steps, separate modalities - show without telling
   - Show the child exactly how you expect the chore to be done.
   - Make a checklist of steps (use pictures or short words).
   - Have fun - the more fun you are having the more solid the learning
2. Start on the last step or in the middle of the chore first to keep it informal and not so overwhelming. Build from that point backwards or forward.
3. Set up playful inspection checkpoints "Inspect what you expect."

Things to remember

1. Poor impulse control is a brain injury issue and frustrating behaviors are most likely not intentional.
   - Keep your cool and refrain from yelling.
   - Why? Because the child is more than likely not misbehaving, but unable to understand certain things.
2. The child may not be able to do two things at once. For example: If you are eating or playing a game the child may not be able to talk.
3. The child may not be able to use their feet and hands at the same time.
4. View behavior problems as a disability that can be dealt with, rather than disobedience.
5. Think stretched toddler, our child may look like other children their age, but trust us when we tell you supervision issues, responsibility issues and amount of freedom. It is for your protection and our child's safety.

Tips on communicating with a child with FASD

1. Find a quiet place to talk. Why? Large, noisy and busy areas are hard to communicate and function well in.
   - Turn off radio or TV.
   - Close door.
   - Move to quieter area.
   - Hang a do not disturb sign
2. Began talking with simple topics.
   - How is your dog?
   - What did you eat for lunch?
   - Talk about things the child likes.
   - Stay on one topic.
3. State one sentence at a time.
   - Make it easy for the child to participate in a conversation by asking yes and no questions.
   - Remain still or walk at the same speed as the child when talking.
   - Keep sentences short.
   - Instead of asking why, use words like where, how, what, who or when. Why will send their brain in a house of mirrors.
4. Allow time for child to respond, refrain from hurrying child.
   - If our child can not get the right word, don't fill in, give clues or description or ask the child to point.
   - Repeat a point using different words.
   - Keep information simple but don't talk down to the child
   - Do not use baby talk
5. Give them choices to ease decision making, but still allow independence of choice.
6. Be an active listener.
   - Give frequent eye contact.
   - Look for gestures.
   - If understanding is unclear, take a guess (are you talking about . . . Oh now I get it.)
7. Look through the child's eyes.
   - How we look at things or understand things may be totally different from how they understand something.
   - Consider watching Forrest Gump with Tom Hanks to get an idea of concrete thinking. For example if you tell   our child to han-

dle it, they may only think about touching it.

8. Share with us and others if you learn better ways to talk with our child so all can benefit.

9. Avoid behavior which winds our child up. Such as tickling, wrestling and pillow fighting.

10. Sit or squat next to our child, do not stand over.

11. In a group, make sure the child is placed so conversation can be around them.

12. May not be able to express needs such as thirst, hunger, going to toilet and may fidget instead.

Controlled successes

Provide opportunities for your child to succeed.

- A carnival game that allows every child to win.
- Visit to the amusement park on Mother's Day when all the other mother's are doing something else and there are no crowds.
- Short periods of time at an event and then leave to integrate child in regular community life -
  - Circus to see the lions.
  - Sunday worship and leave before service.
  - Parade to see one marching band
  - Museum to see dinosaurs.
  - Library to get one book.
  - Restaurant to have desert.
  - Grocery shopping to get less then ten items
- Set an attainable goal and break into very small steps and show progress to a larger goal on a posted chart with stickers

Controlled failures

- We allow our child to fail at times so that she/he learns the consequences.
  We offer Plan A and Plan B.
  —Plan A allows the child to do it the way he chooses.
  —Plan B provides another way to handle a situation.
  We role play both plans. We discovered 'real life' experiences provided better opportunity to make a permanent memory, so sometimes we allow him to try his way and fail. Once the choice is made, we provide the supports to help him learn from his choice.

Mak's seven-step process to teach Liz new skills.

1. REVIEW — We review the options of how to teach so we have a backup plan. We make the initial calls, visit the site and discover the details.

2. WATCH — We tell Liz what she is going to learn and take her through the process to accomplish the task. In this first step she is the observant participant with us — we do not require learning.

3. WATCH — EXPERIENCE We repeat the experience with her contributing pieces of the learned task.

4. EXPERIENCE — WATCH We repeat the experience with her contributing more pieces of the learned task and we begin to step away.

5. EXPERIENCE — SHOW — She tells me what to do and I laugh and become a partner in "her" learning.

6. SHOW — LET GO — She shows me as I watch and then let go.

7. I CAN — She skillfully and a bit fearfully completes the process, while I sit in a parking lot waiting or stay close to the phone to guide. 'I Can', can take a while and when learning is mastered we move on to the Next Step in our adult journey.

QUOTES TO HELP YOU UNDERSTAND

"You can only buy something under $10."

An arm load of new clothes later, the teen assumes you will purchase all she has found as long as each is under $10.00.

"Why does the counselor want to me ride in a wagon when I am mad?"

An anger management specialist had recently described that emotions ebb and flo like waves. You need to ride them up and then ride the wave back down. Being from the midwest and no used to wave action, the conversation was understood as a wagon. The changing weather and movement of clouds would have been a better visual.

FASD RESOURCES FOR FAMILIES FROM FAMILIES

ABC's of Back to School with FASD From a mother's heart

By Kari Fletcher written for her son's teacher (used with permission)

A. Alcohol. My child was exposed to alcohol before birth.

B. Brain. Alcohol use during pregnancy can permanently damage the child's brain.

C. Corpus Callosum. The part of the brain that passes information between the left side (rules) and the right side (impulses) may be damaged or absent with FASD.

D. DSI-Dysfunction of Sensory Integration. My child is sometimes sensitive to florescent lights, tags on clothing, visual over-stimulation, noises, smells, etc…

E. Emotional. My child can be very emotional and often has a low frustration tolerance.

F. Fetal Alcohol Spectrum Disorders (FASD), the "umbrella term" for the damage done when alcohol is used during pregnancy.

G. Give my child praise when he does something well or when he tries hard.

H. Hyperactivity. My child might have a hard time sitting for long periods of time.

I. Immaturity. Because of his FASD, my child may often act half his age.

J. Judgment. My child may exhibit poor judgment. This is from the damage to the frontal lobe of his brain and because of this he needs supervision and lots of reminders.

K. Kindness and redirection is far more effective than punishment.

L. Learn. My child CAN learn but learns differently.

M. Mental retardation. FASD is the #1 cause of mental retardation in North America but most people with FASD have IQs within the normal range.

N. National Organization on Fetal Alcohol Syndrome (www.nofas.org)—visit their website as well as those of their state affiliates! (www.mofas.org for Minnesota)

O. Other drugs. "Of all the substances of abuse, including heroin, cocaine, and marijuana, alcohol produces by far the most serious neuro behavioral effects in the fetus, resulting in life-long permanent disorders of memory function, impulse control and judgment." (Institute of Medicine 1996 Report to Congress)

P. Parenting. My child's behaviors may appear, to those who do not understand FASD, to be the result of poor parenting. Please be slow to blame and quick to consult me.

Q. Quiet time to regroup. My child has problems with self-regulation and may need a quiet time and space to calm down. Providing this will reduce unwanted behaviors.

R. Repetition. Memory issues are very frustrating for my child, repeat and re-teach often.

S. Sleep disorders. My child often has trouble sleeping, please understand if he is tired.

T. Time. Time is an abstract concept and my child does not "feel" it like you and I do.

U. Understanding. Understanding that my child has a disability rather than trying to change something he cannot control will make both his life and yours a lot easier!

V. Visual. Many people with FASD learn best with visual and hands-on type lessons.

W. Willful. Behaviors may appear willful…remind yourself often of the brain damage!

X. X-ample. My child needs examples of good behavior and appropriate role models.

Y. You will make a difference in my child's life. It is my prayer that it is a positive one.

Z. Zero alcohol during pregnancy. Please help me spread the word that FASD is 100% preventable!

I discovered embryology was not a subject to which a great deal of attention was given in medical school. This made me wonder if perhaps many unsolved medical mysteries had their roots in this period of greatest learning, most rapid growth, and greatest vulnerability. When the body is first learning how to be a body and the brain is learning the vast majority of what it will know about being a brain.

Julie Motz (1998)

Secondary disabilities

(May developed as a result of failure to properly deal with the primary disabilities.)

- Learning disabilities
- Early school drop-out
- Depression
- Social problems
- Behavioral problems
- Prostitution
- Sexual acting out
- Juvenile delinquency

- Reactive outbursts
- Suicide
- Mental Illness
- Homelessness
- Addiction
- Early pregnancy
- Chronic unemployment

- Poverty
- Violence
- Alcoholism
- Crimes against property
- Promiscuity

Sources for both charts: Striessguth, Malbin, Moores, Ritchie.

Most sorrowfully, we found that the combination of their superficially good verbal skills and their behavior problems made them unacceptable candidates for most traditional treatment programs. The girls were often teenage mothers, the boys in trouble with the law... Ann Striessguth, Ph.D.

10 Steps of Moving Beyond Secondary Disabilities

I had hoped in our family's work during Liz's teen years we would avoid the secondary disabilities associated with FASD. Out of the twenty listed outcomes our daughter experienced fifteen of them in the three years of transition to adulthood. What could we have changed?

1. Get a diagnosis earlier and begin brain reorganization and sensory integration work before age five.

2. Realize in the beginning we are raising an adult and regardless of differences build a skill base for adult living.

3. Create more healthy adult relationships for her as a youth that would braid into her adulthood and provide wholesome activities.

4. Give her time to process as she is learning, realizing that the way she experiences the world is vastly different from the world I work, live and participate.

5. Utilize her learning strengths of being shown versus being told. Provide experience in step-by-step skills and time to practice—one step at a time—until confidence is gained.

6. Understand and accept it is a brain based injury and day-to-day life is complex and gets more complex in adulthood.

7. Develop a safety plan with skills training beginning by ten years old for managing money, making decisions, remaining safe, seeking help, cooking, cleaning, etc.

8. Seek support services before she was a teen to offer skill building and friendship.

9. Volunteer in the community to build relationships, experience and skills.

10. Continue to provide insight into what we have learned to help the children and families following in our footsteps.

Jodee Kulp

WHAT HAPPENS WHEN ONE FAMILY ADOPTS ANOTHER?
FROM "JUST A MOM" TO "WARRIOR PARENT"

TINY TITAN - JOURNEY OF HOPE
by Ann Yurcek

Book review of Tiny Titan by Susan Rose, President of the Fetal Alcohol Syndrome Support Network of New York City & L.I.

"I'm just a mom", says Ann Yurcek at the beginning of her inspiring book *Tiny Titan*. But after reading about all the obstacles that this mother has had to fight to help her children, the reader is in awe of Ann and knows that "This is no ordinary mom". *Tiny Titan* is filled with treasures to uplift those have been challenged or overwhelmed by life. Through adversity we watch Ann, her husband, and her children become wiser and stronger. Yurcek's gift to us is to share her insights so that we, too, have the opportunity to gain wisdom, to become more deeply spiritual, and to make a difference.

The Yurcek family is a success story. But *Tiny Titan* is not the end of Ann Yurcek's vision. She and her children have already made progress in changing the 'system' in their state. Some other states are beginning to make changes in their medical, mental health, and foster care systems as a result of Ann Yurcek's efforts. It is now up to us to follow her example. Take the first step. Read *Tiny Titan*. Begin a journey that has the ability to enrich and empower all of us.

TINY TITAN - ONE SMALL GIFT

was republished as an e-book for 2012 National Heart Month and given to over 500 readers as a gift in celebration of Becca's 21st year of life.

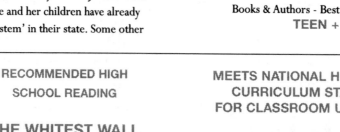

2008 Gold Mom's Choice - Best Adult Non-Fiction

2008 Gold Mom's Choice - Most Inspirational

5 Star Dove Award

Books & Authors - Best Inspirational
TEEN +

RECOMMENDED HIGH SCHOOL READING

THE WHITEST WALL
OTLEG BROTHERS
BOOK ONE
- NOVEL -
by Jodee Kulp

The Whitest Wall has the ability to change the perception of how we view others, treat others and understand others. Learning how to deal with brain injuries, neurodevelopmental therapies and living with a neurologic brain condition, is life threatening for many. Without the proper support, understanding or human connection, these injured beings fall from everyday life. Sometimes these injuries are not always heard or seen and people live in a silent world of pain. Kulp's novel, *The Whitest Wall* , opens the door to the silence and screams to promote insight.

— Sara Hassler, *Midwest Book Review*

MEETS NATIONAL HIGH SCHOOL CURRICULUM STANDARDS FOR CLASSROOM USE - TEEN +

"Kulp has created a new third-person *Catcher in the Rye*"
— Lyelle Palmer, Ph.D., Special Education Professor Emeritus, Winona State University, MN

"Jodee Kulp's beautifully drawn characters will touch your heart, mind and soul."
— bestselling author, Diane Chamberlain, *Before The Storm*

The Whitest Wall has received the following awards:

BOOK 2
COMING 2013

- 2009 Gold Mom's Choice - Best Adult Non-Fiction
- 2009 Gold Mom's Choice - Best Young Adult Non-Fiction
- 2012 Best USA Books Fiction - Young Adult

NOW AVAILABLE & AFFORDABLE CURRICULUM FOR DAY CARE, FAMILIES and HEADSTART PROGRAMS

S.M.A.R.T. Pre-K

Ages 3, 4 & 5

Making brain training FUN!
www.actg.org

You can help your child in brain readiness and have fun together.

A Chance To Grow (ACTG) promotes the maximum development of the whole child through innovative, individualized and comprehensive brain-centered programs and services. These services are educational, therapeutic and rehabilitative in nature. Over the past decade and a half, ACTG has worked with elementary school teachers to introduce the S.M.A.R.T. curriculum (Stimulating Maturity through Accelerated Readiness Training) into elementary school daily instruction. The S.M.A.R.T. curriculum provides brain stimulation for improved learning readiness, literacy and math skills. ACTG has trained over 4,000 teachers in twelve states.

Over the five years, ACTG was able to demonstrate that:
- The S.M.A.R.T. curriculum can be adapted to a preschool setting **and can be used in the home!**
- Teachers can learn, accept, and support this new tool;
- Head Start children receiving S.M.A.R.T. – E.C. generally perform better on tests of early literacy skills and school readiness measures than those who do not receive it;
- Head Start children who received S.M.A.R.T. – E.C. entered kindergarten ready to learn and at a level equal to national norms;
- As Head Start/S.M.A.R.T. – E.C. students progressed through K-2 grades, they continued to learn at levels expected of all students;
- There was no evidence of a "fade" in later grades—the Head Start/S.M.A.R.T. – E.C. students continued to perform at the normative level through Grade 2.

S.M.A.R.T. stands for

Stimulating

Maturity through

Accelerated

Readiness

Training

INPUT Instruction

First, the teacher gives 8 - 10 inputs.
After 8-10 inputs the brain
MAY be ready for an output.
Learn more at:

www.actg.org

S.M.A.R.T. Pre-K provides brain stimulating activities to help bring children up to or beyond their age level and prepare them to learn prior to entering elementary school. This is a great opportunity for our children with FASD!

Together, Karl, Jodee and their daughter, Liz Kulp and now Sam, work to build awareness and help professionals and families utilize strategies to support young people and adults with this often hidden disability. Liz, Sam, Karl and/or Jodee speak to schools, churches, prisons, and treatment centers, in addition to sharing at conferences.

Live Abilities, their new program designed for adults takes the 'dis out to change outcomes is a fun upbeat strategy to help adults find purposely living opportunities while living withe the challenges of FASD. Through braided cord strategies, training of trail guides and learning to mark trails for success this new team reaches our into another pioneering area—to build success for adults.

They currently live in the Midwest and travel as a team to build understanding for prevention and help professionals and families with strategies of support for persons living with FASDs.

———————

For more information visit www.betterendings.org.

For family support information visit www.toolboxparent.com

For adult and transition support information visit www.braidedcord.net

For speaking contact: jodeekulp@gmail.com | subject: Presentations

Follow us on Twitter @*SilentVoices* | Facebook @*Better Endings*

CPSIA information can be obtained at www.ICGtesting.com
Printed in the USA
LVOW09s1806221013

358078LV00005B/858/P